# I Survived

## VICTORIA CILLIERS

PAN BOOKS

First published 2020 by Pan Books
an imprint of Pan Macmillan
The Smithson, 6 Briset Street, London EC1M 5NR
Associated companies throughout the world
www.panmacmillan.com

ISBN 978-1-5290-2037-3

5 7 9 8 6 4

A CIP catalogue record for this book is available from the British Library.

Typeset by Palimpsest Book Production Limited,
Falkirk, Stirlingshire
Printed and bound by CPI Group (UK) Ltd, Croydon, CR0 4YY

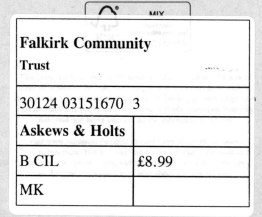

For my parents, who have always supported me regardless of the challenges life has thrown at us, and my children, who I love to the moon and back.

# Contents

# Prologue

*Oh god*, I thought. *I don't want to do this.* I was a professional jumper with thousands of jumps behind me, but this would be my first skydive in over a year and, as the small plane climbed, everything felt familiar but it also felt wrong. My mind kept wandering to my two babies waiting for me at home. April was almost three years old and Ben was only five weeks. *I should be with them, not here.*

The jump had been my husband Emile's idea, something we could do together, he'd said, which is mainly why I agreed. I also thought it would prove one way or another whether I still enjoyed skydiving, or whether I should give up my role as an instructor.

In the end Emile didn't join me as he couldn't find anyone to look after the children, but he'd encouraged me to jump by myself.

I rose from my seat in the small aircraft as it circled above the airfield, and clambered to the open door near the tail. The jumper in front of me leapt from the plane and disappeared into the clouds. Now alone, I crouched by the exit, strapping my helmet up tightly. Sound engulfed the plane in a roar of engine and wind, and my nerves bubbled. Still, I couldn't back out now. *Just get on with it*, I told myself. *Then you can go home.*

My helmet was strapped in place with the visor lowered over my eyes, but I gave it one last tug to make sure it wouldn't budge. Below the plane was a 3,000-foot drop and as I stared down, searching through the clouds, I spotted the airfield. It looked like a dot on the ground and I started to feel sick. I held my breath, waiting until the previous jumper was far enough away. *It's now or never*, I decided. Pausing for a split-second, I pushed my fears to the back of my mind. Without another thought, I jumped.

The cold air hit my face and immediately I felt calm. *I know what I'm doing*, I thought, letting the relief wash over me. Expertly, I spread my arms out in front of me, maintaining control of the fall, and with my right hand I reached for the parachute strapped to my back. I found the toggle at the base of the rig and pulled down, deploying the parachute. Its canopy billowed out above me but instead of slowing me down, I felt an uneven jolt.

*That's odd*, I thought, looking up. I was shocked to see that the lines keeping me tied to the parachute were twisted. *This is nothing I haven't fixed before*, I told myself, and immediately my mind went into autopilot. I kicked through the air in a circular motion, skilfully unravelling the ropes. As they came free I felt a second of relief, quickly replaced by horror.

*I'm still not slowing down.*

I tried releasing the brake lines and pulling hard on the opposing riser to the spin, but that didn't help either. It didn't make sense. My eyes were fixed on the parachute above me, willing it to cooperate, but no matter what I did, I couldn't control the violent spinning. When none of the solutions my training had taught me seemed to work, I knew what I had to do. *I'm going to have to cut it away.* It had to be a snap decision. With the ground hurtling closer and closer, I hurriedly pulled the cut-away pad on the harness, detaching the main parachute, and deployed the reserve handle. It was a back-up parachute for emergencies like this and I knew it was the only option now.

I held my breath, preparing for the sudden jolt the reserve would give, but as it opened I felt nothing. I snapped my eyes up. The reserve had only half inflated and now I was spinning wildly. The parachute threw me across the sky until I was almost upside down. I tugged at the risers, trying desperately to gain some control. *The children need me*, I thought. *I have to sort this out.* But it was no use. Plummeting helplessly, still pulling down on the risers, fighting to survive, all my attention was focused upwards. I had no idea how far I was from the ground.

# 1

# The Army

'Why don't you tag along and see what the army's about, Vicky?' my friend Kate said.

She was going to an officer training presentation for the military, aimed at medical and nursing students interested in joining the Royal Army Medical Corps.

I had moved to Glasgow to study physiotherapy at the university there and, while I had been a member of the cadets at school, joining the army as an adult was something I had never seriously considered before now. *It could be fun though*, I thought to myself. I was always keen for new adventures and, at a loose end, I agreed to go along.

As soon as the presentation began, with action shots flashing across the screen, the prospect of excitement and service in the military captured my imagination.

'There are endless opportunities to work in different places,' one of the presenters at the front of the lecture room told us, flicking through a slideshow of officers treating people around the world. 'Many of our officers end up travelling all over the globe, it's a life-changing experience.'

*What if I did join the army? Where would it take me?* I knew already that my dad would be supportive. Both of his parents had experience of military service and he would be so proud if I carried on the family tradition. Watching the gallery of pictures flick past, I imagined the fast-paced life of the army and what it would be like in training, learning military skills and going on operations. It would be a far cry from my loving and comfortable childhood.

I was born in Edinburgh's Western General Hospital in 1975. My mum was Scottish and my dad was from Devon. They met in the students' union at Edinburgh where my mum was a nursing student and my dad was studying to be an actuary. My childhood had been reassuringly normal. Mum and Dad had a warm but disciplined approach to parenting. At a push, I would probably say I was a daddy's girl, but not notably so – I adored both Mum and Dad and the happy life they'd created for me. Mum gave up her job as a nurse to stay home and bring me up, while Dad went out to work (he started as a programmer for Standard Life and worked his way up to an information systems development manager). When my little brother Christopher came along four years after me, we became the perfect nuclear family who all sat down to dinner every evening. Haddington, some twenty miles east of Edinburgh, was a quiet town in the eighties and we could be left safely to our own devices. Busy with school and activities in the week, I filled my weekends with horse riding. I absolutely loved the horses, figuring I could quite easily spend my entire life tending to them. I was a secure and well-balanced child who couldn't imagine that anything would threaten life as I knew it. It wasn't until I was fourteen years old that my first taste of heartbreak arrived.

'What is going on with Mum and Dad?' I asked Christopher one day, cornering him in the living room. He simply shrugged.

'Who knows,' he replied, not seeming to take much notice of the change in the house. 'It's probably nothing.'

I wanted to believe him, but I had suspected something wasn't right for weeks. It was as though the whole house swelled with an unspoken secret. My parents seemed unusually quiet as we sat round the dinner table, and I'd catch them sharing knowing glances and whispering when Christopher and I were out of earshot. One day I saw Dad muttering something to my mum by the half-open bedroom door. He saw me and closed it completely. *Something is definitely going on*, I thought, unable to ignore how carefully they were keeping us from reality.

Despite this, I tried my best to brush it aside, choosing to ignore the niggling feeling inside my head. *There's nothing I can do about it if they're not going to tell me*, I reminded myself, and so I decided to play along with them. In the safe haven of our family home, I was so content with our life in Haddington and, terrified of anything bursting our little bubble, I was more than happy to assume everything was fine until told otherwise. It was the only way I knew how to cope, to pretend everything was normal. Eventually, though, that too was shattered when one Saturday morning Mum and Dad came into my room to wake me up, and I finally discovered the devastating truth.

'Morning, Victoria,' Dad said softly, perching himself at the end of my bed. 'We need to talk to you.' I heard the tone in his voice and my stomach began to do flips. I knew whatever it was, it would be something I didn't want to hear.

'Sure,' I replied, sitting up in my bed. I wrapped my arms around myself protectively, bracing for what was to come.

'We were hoping we wouldn't have to tell you this, but we think it's time for you to know,' Dad began to say, and I noticed his head lowering as he spoke. 'Your mum has cancer.'

The news swooped in like a punch to my stomach and for the first time, I had a dizzy feeling in my head. *This isn't happening.* Of all my theories of what could have been wrong, this was ten times worse. It felt as though the bottom of my world was about to fall out.

'Oh,' I mumbled, frozen in place, my face still. My mind raced but I was at a loss for what to say.

'We're not sure what the prognosis is yet,' Dad continued, looking up at me. 'But she's going to get treatment.'

'Treatment?' I asked, confused by all of the information being thrown at me.

'Chemotherapy, Victoria,' Mum chimed in, giving me a quick smile. 'They're hoping it will fight off the cancer.' My eyes flicked from Mum to Dad and both of them stared back, waiting for me to react, but I still didn't flinch. My body had gone into shock and I retreated into myself in the face of such a huge emotional obstacle. (It was the first but not the last time this would happen.) On the inside, however, the thought of my mum having cancer was almost too much to bear. I had so many questions, but I had no idea where to begin. *Do I even want to know the answers?* I wondered.

The emotional pain pricked my skin like goosebumps, but I did my best to remain calm and collected. *What good would it do for Mum to see me cry?* I thought, determined to stay strong. *That would only make things worse.*

Christopher, who was only ten, was too young to fully understand what was happening, but I later learnt it was bowel cancer that was making Mum poorly, and that during a routine operation to remove her appendix, the doctors had discovered the true extent of her condition. I was devastated.

I coped with the news the only way I knew how, and that was to distance myself from it all. *There's no point in dwelling on it*, I told myself, wishing but never really believing it was that simple. *The doctors will get rid of the cancer.*

The initial surgery was followed by bouts of chemotherapy. Each time we were all hopeful that it would be good news and my parents always tried to stay positive for me and my brother, but it took a toll on us all. I felt that I just had to get through the days, weeks and months, and that it would be fine in the end. I never let myself believe that she might die and that was never directly suggested to Christopher and me. I took up additional hobbies at school to immerse myself and distract my thoughts. I joined the army cadets and started drumming. I was the first ever female side drummer in the school's Pipes and Drums band. I got heavily into rock and metal music and would spend all my free time listening to tapes of Metallica and Nirvana. Music, drumming and horse riding were my escape. The teachers at school knew about my mum, as did my best friend Catriona, but they didn't broach the topic unless I did. A couple of times my emotions got the better of me at school, and I remember sitting in a study period when I just couldn't stop the tears. I kept turning up my music but it wouldn't drown out the pain. Catriona wrapped her arms around me and held me until it stopped. But aside from the occasional blip, I outwardly presented a 'normal' persona to the world.

In between her regular appointments and gruelling procedures, Mum was resilient. She would come home from the hospital and pick up with normal life where she had left off, continuing to make our school lunches and carry on as best she could. It was no use though. After a couple of years, my parents decided it was time to head off on what Dad referred to as our last family holiday.

'If it's the last time we're all together,' Dad announced to Christopher and me, 'we want to make sure we create some happy memories.' Each word Dad used to describe the trip made me feel sicker than the last.

'I don't want to go,' I blurted out before I could stop myself, and I watched in horror as my mum's face fell. I felt awful.

'But we're going to Hawaii,' she tried to coax me, and that only made me feel worse. 'You'll have a lovely time.' I knew this was going to be hard for them as I shook my head in disagreement.

'I can't go,' I replied, feeling numb. The idea of a family vacation with my parents did sound wonderful but knowing it would be our last was too devastating to think about. *I'm not ready to say goodbye*, I realized. The thought of going along felt like I would be accepting Mum's fate. *If I don't go, she can't die*. I was struggling to comprehend the reality of her situation and, for me, the most pragmatic solution was to ignore it altogether.

'What are you going to do while we're away then?' Dad asked, but I already had an idea in mind.

'There's an equestrian camp this summer,' I told them. 'I could go there instead.' Just by the looks on their faces I knew my parents were heartbroken, and I felt terrible but I would not change my mind. They must have realized this was my way of coping and ultimately they respected my wishes. I waved them off as Mum, Dad and Christopher headed to the airport, a small sinking feeling settling into my stomach as the car pulled out of the drive. *What else could I do?* I thought to myself. I couldn't take Mum's cancer away and the thought of losing her petrified me.

Deep down we all knew there was no hope, and within weeks of returning from their dream holiday, Dad had more bad news to break to me.

'We're going to have to move your mum to a hospice.' At the time, 'hospice' seemed synonymous with hospital to me and so, watching as the health assistants helped her into her room, I had no idea that there was no hope of her ever coming home again. I don't think I completely understood, or perhaps I chose not to understand what was going on, but either way I pretended this was all a normal part of the cancer treatment. We visited Mum as much as we could and on one of our trips to see her, she took me by surprise when she asked what I planned to do with my life.

'Um,' I hesitated, caught off guard. I had always loved the idea of becoming a vet, doing call-outs to different farms and stables and rescuing injured animals, but I knew my grades weren't up to scratch. 'Being a physio seems interesting.' The answer hadn't been plucked out of nowhere. I was completely mad about horse riding and so I figured my keen interest in the equine world could be put to use by caring for injured horses. But to do that, I would need to study physiotherapy.

'That does sound interesting.' Mum smiled at me from her bed. The question felt daunting but I understood why she'd asked. She wanted the comfort of knowing what direction our lives would take after she was gone. I spent nearly every day with her, quietly noting that each time we went, she seemed weaker and more fragile. Even though the sinking feeling I had told me that she wasn't going to recover, I just couldn't imagine a world without her in it.

It was in September, one month before my sixteenth birthday, when we kissed Mum goodbye. We were all in a state of shock, Dad, Christopher and I, unsure of what life would look like without Mum. For the first few days we were kept busy.

'We're so sorry for your loss,' the constant stream of relatives would mutter, passing over bits of food to help with making our dinner.

'Thank you,' I answered quietly, not knowing what else to say.

My mum's parents came to stay with us for a while, and between entertaining them and helping Dad plan the funeral there wasn't much time to think. The day we laid my mum to rest was, and still is, the hardest emotional event I have ever endured. I tried my best not to cry, willing myself to be strong for the family, but the pain I felt was an all-encompassing physical agony. It was devastating to sit through – I thought my heart would split. Afterwards, the house was flooded with family dropping in to pay their respects, but eventually people stopped coming round and the house fell quiet. That's when reality finally sunk in: it was just the three of us now.

\*    \*    \*

Dad coped with Mum's death the same as I did, the only way either of us could. He retreated into himself, quietly ignoring the fact that there was a place missing at the dinner table.

He was still working full-time and, with no one else to help, I did my best to ease the strain on him. I took over as much as I could, doing the washing and attempting to produce meals after school so he didn't have to, but even so the house felt segregated. Christopher would retreat to his room, Dad would be doing his own thing, and we didn't come together much as a family. My escape became the music room at school and, spending as much time there as I could, I threw myself into drumming, both for the pipe band and playing along to tapes of heavy metal bands. While I wasn't sure if the other pupils were aware of what had happened, the teachers let me be, giving me the occasional sympathetic glance if I passed them in the corridor.

One day, I was on my way to drum practice when I noticed a poster hanging on the school wall. *Partake in a Charity Parachute Jump* it read, and instantly I knew I wanted to do it. *This is exactly the kind of escape I need*, I thought, eager for any activity to lose myself in. It was the promise of something entirely different, something fun. I noted the details of the first meeting in the corner of the poster and, taking my seat in the school hall that afternoon, I couldn't wait to sign myself up. I already knew which charity I wanted to support – to raise money for bowel cancer research in memory of my mum.

More than sixty pupils attended that very first meeting, but when the day of our jump finally came, it was just the five of us that piled into an Austin Metro borrowed from one of the parents. We all drove down from Edinburgh to Nottingham and it felt like my first real adventure away from home. I laughed and joked with the other students as we made our way across the country, a mixture of nerves and anticipation fluttering in my stomach. I had always been reasonably fearless as a kid – all of the horse riding had taught me to relish adrenaline – and I fizzed with excitement at the thought of jumping out of a plane. As we drove up to Langar Airfield, I peered out at the small aircraft parked in the distance and felt apprehensive for the first time. *I don't think I've ever seen a plane that small.* Dad had told me how much fun the jumps he'd done when he was younger were, and so I thought to myself, *let's give it a go*, letting any mild nerves vanish from my mind.

'We're here,' our driver announced, and without hesitation we all bounded out of the car.

'You'll be staying in the bunkhouse,' a member of staff said, greeting us at reception before showing us to our cabin at the parachute centre. The evening was spent socializing, but that night my stomach flipped with nerves and excitement so I couldn't sleep, and by the next morning I was exhausted. We went down to the airfield after breakfast to attend some ground schooling and then, with our equipment ready to go, we heaved on our kit before heading out to the aircraft. We would be doing a tandem skydive and had each been assigned an instructor to jump with. Boarding the plane, I was jittery with anticipation. At first everyone seemed giddy, excitedly chatting with one another as the plane took off, but the higher the plane flew, the quieter we became.

'OK,' one of the instructors called out once the plane had levelled. 'Everyone ready?' He had to shout over the noise of the propellers and I strained to hear him. A few people gave him a thumbs-up and, one by one, our instructors shuffled us towards the open door. I was petrified as I hovered over the edge of the plane. I could see the sandy circle where I'd be landing, in a patch of green grass surrounded by yellow wheat fields. The smell of aviation fuel washed in and time seemed to slow down. There was a moment of calmness, waiting for what was to come. *It's too late to back out now*, I thought in a last-minute panic. But the second I tipped forward, leaving the aircraft, all of my anxiety washed away. It was amazing. The icy air rushed past me, almost burning the sides of my face, and right then, a couple of thousand feet above any of life's worries, I felt utter freedom. It was euphoric. We fell freely for a few seconds before a sharp jolt snapped us out of the air and the parachute opened. When we landed safely on the ground, the adrenaline rush kicked in and immediately I wanted to go back up and do it again.

'That was incredible,' I gushed to the other students, the group of us excited by what we had just accomplished. *I could happily do this every day*, I thought to myself, the spark of a new passion lighting up. That evening, when the car pulled out of the parachute centre to take us back to Scotland, I felt a sense of sadness. I envied the instructors. *They have such a cool job*, I thought, wishing I could have stayed there to learn the ropes. But I was seventeen, with no real disposable income – it was unrealistic to expect I'd ever jump again.

Four years later, as I listened to the army officer's training presentation, I thought back to my skydiving experience. The adrenaline rush was still so vivid in my mind and I imagined a similar feeling being part of the armed forces, especially during a conflict.

'Have you ever considered joining the army?' one of the speakers asked me at the end of the presentation. Kate had wandered off to the bar and I was standing alone, looking through the leaflets for the military.

'No, I'm training to be a physio,' I admitted. 'Is there even a place for physios in the army?'

'Absolutely,' he replied, and handed me a card with a contact number on it. 'Get in touch if you want to schedule an interview.' I took the card and gave the presenter a smile before going to find my friend. After that evening, the notion of a new opportunity, a new escape, stayed with me.

On paper, I had it all together. I had secured a postgraduate job at a local hospital, I had a few close friends that I regularly spent time with, I was living with my boyfriend – and I was ever so slightly bored. *I want to do something with my life*, I thought, horrified by how everything seemed to be mapped out for me. Itching to start afresh, I had already looked into working as a physio abroad but now, with the idea of joining the army planted in the back of my mind, I knew I had to leave Glasgow. *I'll just see if I get in first*, I resolved, signing up to attend an interview. *It can't be easy to get picked.* I imagined endless months of waiting before never hearing back, but a few weeks later I clutched my acceptance letter in my hand: the escape I had been searching for.

*Can I really just up and leave?* I wondered, but I already knew the answer and, while breaking the news to my boyfriend was difficult, I knew I was making the right decision. It would be six months before I could join up, so after my degree I worked at the local hospital until the time came for me to pack everything I owned into the back of my Nissan Micra and drive down south, leaving everyone and everything else behind.

I knew the job awaiting me would be full of excitement, but nothing could have prepared me for how quickly I would be thrown into the deep end. I started my initial training at Keogh Barracks in Aldershot, where we were taught the basics. Our kit was issued, and we were instructed how to iron and wear it properly. There were endless drills and lessons on army doctrine. It was an essential course for anyone joining who already had qualifications, to learn more about how the army worked. Then it was on to Sandhurst, where I began a basic infantry course.

Royal Military Academy Sandhurst was as intimidating but also as thrilling as I had imagined. From day one it was tough. Very tough. We had the trade skills, but the staff had to assess whether we had the strength of character to be an officer. There was a packed schedule, with constant physical activity, minimal breaks and limited sleep. At least I formed strong friendships with my peers, which would be key in helping us cope in the more stressful conditions of operational tours.

We were allowed one telephone call a week, and I remember calling my dad when I was at an all-time low – sleep-deprived, hungry and fed up of being constantly shouted at. I seemed to be on all the weekend duties and felt like the kicking ball of my platoon colour sergeant, a short squat Welsh guardsman. My dad was incensed at his daughter seemingly being bullied and sworn at, and it was all I could do to stop him calling the staff and giving them a piece of his mind. That would really not have helped my situation!

'Once you're in the army, you're an officer first and your trade comes second,' one of the training officers told us at Sandhurst. 'So it is vital for you to learn what is required of soldiers and how to function both in camp and out on tour.'

The months of training, learning more about military medicine, infantry skills, leadership and weapon handling, went by in a blur and before long it was the passing out parade. By this time Dad had married Frances and both were at the parade to watch me. Everyone who had completed training was allowed to put forward their preferences for where they wanted to be posted. I hoped to be sent somewhere further north, a bit closer to Scotland and my dad, so when I saw where they were sending me, my heart sank.

'Oh no,' I groaned. 'Not HMS *Drake*.'

HMS *Drake* was a naval base in Plymouth and it hadn't even been on my list of preferences. *That's got to be the furthest from home they could have possibly placed me while still being on the same piece of land*, I sighed to myself, but I had no choice.

In Plymouth, I went to work for 3 Commando Brigade, part of the Royal Marines. At first, I felt out of my depth. I had just spent months learning about the army and now I had been sent onto a naval base where everything was slightly different. While I was still excited about another move, living at the base I felt isolated. I worked part-time on the naval base and part-time at Derriford Hospital and, returning to the mess after my shifts, it was usually quiet. Homesick for my friends and family, the loneliness crept in, but I forced myself to keep busy and as it turned out I wasn't at Derriford for long. After seven months, the army moved me to a new placement in Aldershot to start on New Year's Day. Arriving at the garrison mess sometime over the Christmas period, I expected the place to be a ghost town, but it was full of hospital staff who had been on duty over the holidays. I marvelled at the festivities taking place, a far cry from the quiet base I'd just left. To get to my room,

I needed to go past the bar area, but as I shuffled along with my bag, suddenly I heard someone calling my name.

'Over here, Vicky!' I turned to find a group of people that had been on my course in Keogh Barracks. 'Come drink with us.'

It was about twenty-four hours before I actually made it to my room, and from then on life in the military was much more fun. I lived with all the military hospital staff and that, combined with the fact 5 Airborne Brigade were in Aldershot at the time, meant there were a lot of parties and nights out to attend. I also met a young man in logistics named Brett who lived in the same mess as me and ended up in the same party group. He was fun to be with, happy to give any new experience a go, but also very kind and caring. It was the first serious relationship for both of us.

I was placed at Frimley Park Hospital where I felt I was starting to find my feet. Frimley Park was one of the few Ministry of Defence Hospital Units, an NHS hospital with a military wing. It's vital for military healthcare workers to keep their skills up when not deployed and I spent six months on the intensive care ward, then the military orthopaedic ward. I loved being back in an army environment, working at the hospital during the day, running or doing exercise after work, then going out and socializing with other people from the mess. But all of that was about to change.

Like everyone in the UK, I'd been watching the news stories about the Balkans conflict. In June 1999, 1 Para

Battle Group – as part of 5 Airborne Brigade – were deployed to North Macedonia, where they waited for two weeks at the Kosovo border for the call to move forward. There was a lot of tension in Aldershot just prior to them deploying, as the word was that they might be doing an operational parachute jump. This never happened in the end, and they were inserted by helicopter to secure the road to Pristina, the capital of Kosovo. After two years of fighting, a peace plan had been brokered between Serbia, who controlled the country, and Kosovan Albanians who wanted independence. Serbian troops were withdrawing, and the paras were sent as part of a NATO force to keep peace in a bitterly divided country. And now I was going to Kosovo too, as part of 22 Field Hospital. Although I was nervous about what lay ahead, I couldn't wait to get started. *This is the first time I'll actually get to do the job I signed up to do*, I realized. I felt ready for the challenge that awaited us.

We flew over in a Hercules, a military aircraft designed for the armed forces, and as I stepped off the plane at Skopje airport, the overwhelming dry heat hit me. A large bus arrived to take us to our base, and as we set off we passed a land mine at the side of the road. *We're not playing at being in the army any more*, I thought as our surroundings began to sink in. The hospital had already sent over an advance party from the UK who had set up in Lipljan, a small town in east Kosovo. The military had commandeered a building beside a local prison, not an ideal location as it turned out. As soon as we arrived, I was shown to the ward I'd be working on. The space looked like a large gym that had been converted to make room for the patients. Three lines of beds ran down the room, one line for the Serbs, one line for the Albanians and one for NATO soldiers, so as to segregate them as best we could.

My four months working in Kosovo were my first real exposure to just how evil people can be. One by one, patients would be rushed into the hospital, the effects of what the Serbs and Albanians were doing to each other etched on their bodies in the form of bullet wounds, bloodied clothes and missing limbs. More often than not it was children who were injured by mines, blown up while they were playing in the fields.

Our accommodation block was a concrete two-storey building with rooms big enough for five or six single bed frames. I was sharing with five nurses I knew, either from basic training or Frimley Park. When we first entered the room we all fell silent. It smelt and it was dirty. There was no glass in the windows so dust was pouring in, and there were suspect brown smears all over the walls. The only water in the block came from a pipe in the toilet. The dirty bed frames had no mattresses. This was to be our home for the indefinite future. We got to work and cleaned it as well as possible with a brush and damp rags. We found some clear plastic and taped it over the windows. We had roll mats and sleeping bags, and strung up some rope to hang our clothes on. Initially there was no electricity or running water, the Serbs having cut off the water supply. Whilst we waited for the Royal Engineers to come in and set up generators and a bore-hole, we used torches and bottled water. We got two bottles a day each for washing, and unlimited drinking water. With temperatures in the forties, it was needed. We soon learnt that getting by was all about making connections and who you knew. Having a boyfriend in logistics came in handy when Brett managed to source us some solar showers, which were a godsend. Warm showers: bliss.

One night, I was startled awake by the trauma alarm blaring across the hospital. Still half asleep, I immediately sprang to life, throwing on my uniform before rushing off to the meeting point within the hospital. I thought I'd find staff preparing to admit crowds of injured civilians, knowing all too well that the alarm could only mean a mass-casualty scenario, but when I arrived there were no new patients in sight.

'The Serbs have got hold of a load of Albanian farmers,' I heard someone say as we waited to find out where we were needed.

'We'll be expecting a lot of casualties then,' someone else replied. I remained silent, on tenterhooks, wanting to know what was happening. This was the job I had been preparing for and I paced around the room, expecting to be called any moment. An hour dragged slowly by.

'All of the non-critical staff can stand down,' a senior member of staff announced at last. 'Go back to bed. The alarm will go off if we need you again.'

Slowly, around half of the staff started to file back out of the room. My role at the hospital was 'P3 Casualty', which meant I treated the walking wounded and therefore was no longer needed for the night. *I guess it's not as bad as they thought*, I decided. With nothing else to do, I retreated to my bed and, lying in silence, I let my thoughts swirl. *If the alarm went off then where are the casualties?* I wondered, confused. Then, suddenly, I heard it. *Pop, pop pop* – the crackling sound of shots going off in the distance. I lay still, straining to listen to the noises. The gunshots rang out again and I bolted upright, ready to run back downstairs if I was needed. But the alarm didn't go off and, a few minutes later, the stand-down signal called across the hospital. My stomach dropped and as the horrible, sick feeling settled, I knew there were going to be no casualties that needed treatment because there were no survivors. The next morning, I would discover that the shots I had listened to were twelve farmers being killed by the Serbs.

That night was an eye-opener, but it was just one of the many tragedies I witnessed that brought home how lucky I was to live in the UK, while the civilians of Kosovo had their lives torn apart on a regular basis. Whenever we went outside the hospital gates we had a vehicle convoy with us and, as a physio, I was required to do regular clinics in other areas of Kosovo. It was easier to send me out with a convoy than try to bring individual soldiers into the hospital to see me, and so it wasn't long before the trips outside became routine. It didn't stop the nerves jittering every time the hospital gates opened though. I kept my rifle with me at all times, the fear of the unknown forcing me to stay alert. And we soon realized that being situated next to a prison was going to bring us added problems, since it acted like a magnet for unpleasant men. Presumably they went to visit friends or relatives inside, then turned their attention to us. When our staff were threatened, the Gurkhas were brought in to provide a more intimidating security presence.

'Look at the destruction,' I remarked to my driver on one of my first trips. From our Land Rover we silently surveyed the ruins of what had once been a thriving village. I had joined the army for greater exposure to the world and to support soldiers, and so I would never wish to change this period of my life, as upsetting as it was at times. We become numb to the world's atrocities when we see them on television and in the media. It is something else to be in amongst it and feel the fear, pain and heartache all around you. It changed the way I saw life and made me appreciate what I have. Nothing I've been through has approached the hardship that I witnessed on tour.

I was halfway through my shift at the hospital one day when a man rushed in with his two nieces, who had survived a horrific attack but were suffering trauma. They were about seven and ten years old. My heart broke as I listened to an interpreter explain their situation.

'She's had surgery on her wrist,' the interpreter reported as the uncle spoke, referring to the older of the two girls. 'She was shot in the arm and survived.' The interpreter paused. 'But the majority of her family was lined up and shot at point-blank range in front of her and her sister.' Her sister had been shot in the shoulder and had limited movement and a hideous scar, but was functioning best of the two.

'Right,' I said, forcing my face not to react to the news. Gently, I touched the older girl's arm, noting the surgery marks on her forearm. 'It looks like she needs some physio work on her wrist.'

Looking the child in the eye, it was incredibly hard not to cry in front of her, but instead I smiled. 'We'll fix you up,' I promised.

Over the next few weeks I discovered the full impact the tragedy was having on the little girl – she refused to talk at all during our sessions. I'd had no training in paediatrics or helping patients cope with psychological trauma, so I went with instinct, making sure she understood what I was going to do before I did it. Her wrist gradually started to move again and she was able to hold items in her hand. It felt like a huge breakthrough when she smiled at me for the first time, and she would nod as I spoke to her but she always remained silent. It was heartbreaking to see what had been done to these children and the effect it had on them. All I wanted was to be able to help them, but I was due to leave the hospital, swapping over with another team.

*Just when I've started to make inroads with her*, I agonized. I desperately wanted to stay and continue to help. This little girl had already lost so many people and I was just starting to gain her trust. I couldn't bear the thought of leaving her behind, but I had no choice. Another field hospital was on its way to replace us. I was coming home.

The transition back to life in the UK was a lot harder than I ever expected it to be. *How am I supposed to go back to a normal life now?* I wondered, suffering tremendously with the guilt of leaving all those injured people behind.

'This queue is ridiculous,' I overheard one woman tut at a crowded supermarket. The remark made the hairs on the back of my neck stand up. Since returning from Kosovo, I couldn't help but notice an anger build up inside whenever I was in a crowded place or shopping centre. Hearing people complain about such trivial stuff made me want to snap. As I listened to the woman continue to moan about the busy supermarket, my blood boiled. I envisioned myself storming up to her, pushing her silly shopping trolley out of the way. *Have you got any idea what's going on right now a few hours away?* I wanted to ask her. *You have no idea how good you've got it.*

It took a few months for that anger to start subsiding. I was forced to put it to the back of my mind when I was promoted to captain and moved to a new posting, this time at the Defence Medical Rehabilitation Centre Headley Court, near Epsom. It was a well-known centre and, with the lead regional rehab unit there too, we had an interesting mix of complex injuries to treat. The job was full-on, with a lot of the patients needing complicated treatment, but by now I was emotionally exhausted.

'I just wish there was something to give me a break from it all,' I mentioned to one of the other physios at the unit.

'Why don't you do some adventure training?' she suggested, taking me by surprise.

'Adventure training?' I asked. I had heard there were such courses, but it wasn't something I had been exposed to in the military because I had mainly been working in hospitals.

'There's a list of different things you can sign up to,' she continued as I mulled it over. 'You should have a look, it's good fun.'

After that conversation, I decided to have a scan through the various courses available. There were hundreds of different sports and activities on offer. *How on earth am I going to pick?* I thought, reading through the endless options when suddenly one caught my eye. *Parachuting.* I thought back to the charity jump I had done at school. *I enjoyed it*, I remembered. *I'll give it another go.* It was an easy snap-decision. I signed up for a two-week course at Weston-on-the-Green in Oxford to try my hand once more at skydiving. Two weeks should have been plenty of time to get lots of jumps in, but from the day I arrived the weather was horrific. As rain pelted the parachute centre for a fourth day running, the jumps were cancelled and so, to entertain us, one of the instructors put on videos of people doing different jumps. The second I saw the clips of jumpers in free fall, I was captivated. They looked like aerial gymnasts, spinning through the air at extreme speeds, and I was stunned by how carefree they seemed.

'Wow, that looks incredible,' I marvelled, watching as the skydivers flew through the air. *I want to stay in this sport until I can do that*, I decided to myself.

When the weather finally did pick up, however, I quickly realized how much I hated skydiving. We started with static line jumping, where one end of a cord is attached to the deployment bag on your back, into which your parachute is packed, and the other to the back of the plane. When you jump out of the plane, the cord becomes tight and pulls your bag away from your parachute, which then opens automatically as you fall. The plane would reach a certain altitude, usually 3,000 feet, and begin to fly in circles, round and round, above the parachute centre until it was safe to exit. The constant circling motion made me sick. There was a sense of panic in the air as the instructors shouted orders, rushing everybody towards the door, and by the time it was my turn to jump, I was absolutely terrified. It was frustrating because I had a goal in mind of what I wanted to achieve, but I was scared and after a few jumps I wasn't progressing, which meant that I felt increasingly anxious on each jump. Only if the first few static line jumps went well could you progress to free fall, leaving just three seconds before you opened your parachute to start with, then falling for longer as you became more skilled.

I didn't know how to move forward with the sport until I spotted one of the weekend instructors, Paul, at the bar one evening and made a beeline for him.

'How are you finding it?' he asked, taking a swig of his beer.

'Not great,' I admitted. 'I'm struggling with the static line,' I added, explaining how stressful I found the nature of the jump. 'Free fall looks so much calmer.'

'Well, why don't you come up first thing in the morning with me?' he offered. 'I'll take you to do a free-fall jump.'

'Really?' I asked, the prospect suddenly giving me hope.

'Sure,' he replied. 'We'll do accelerated free-fall level one, and if you enjoy it then why don't you convert from static line to the AFF system? If you don't like it then just draw a line under it, but at least you will have tried.'

'That sounds great,' I agreed and, true to my word, I met him the next morning. We trained together briefly before taking the first lift of the day up into the clouds. Where the aircraft usually began to circle, it kept climbing, and I was surprised to see the jumpers relax, taking off their helmets to make small talk. The entire atmosphere felt different and by the time we reached an altitude of around 13,000 feet, I was completely calm.

*Everyone looks like they're actually enjoying themselves*, I thought – compared to the static line jumps where everybody would be sitting in silence, scared stiff. I watched in awe as one by one, they all exited the aircraft, leaving me and my two instructors the last ones to jump.

'Ready?' one of them asked and I smiled, nodding eagerly. 'Then let's go.'

I strapped my helmet back on and the instructors practically lifted me into place before the open door. The all-encompassing noise of the wind drowned out any nerves. Both instructors took their spots, each holding on to me. We leapt from the aircraft and immediately I felt euphoria. They kept hold of me for the free-fall element of the jump, until I had deployed the parachute. Any stress or anxiety about skydiving faded away and suddenly I was totally weightless. I laughed as the wind whipped past my face, all sound lost in the air. The feeling I had as we fell was incredible. The only way to possibly describe it is freedom, total and utter freedom. From the second I landed safely on the ground I had a massive grin that would stay plastered on my face for days. As soon as the adrenaline wore off, I ran back into the centre to transfer my classes over to an accelerated free-fall programme. I was completely hooked.

# 2

# Skydiving

Once I was captivated by the world of parachuting, I knew there would be no going back for me. Itching to learn more about the sport and become a more competent skydiver, I spent every spare weekend I had at the parachute centre and soon enough, almost all of my friends and social life revolved around the sport. I loved it.

'Are you staying out tonight, Vicky?' one of the other jumpers asked once we had landed safely on the ground. We had just taken the final lift of the day.

'Of course,' I enthused. 'I wouldn't miss it.'

In the evening, everyone from the parachute centre would drink together, socializing as a group at the weekend with big nights out. I had so much fun, laughing and joking with the other jumpers until the early hours of the morning before staying overnight in the bunkhouse at the airfield, sometimes camping out in tents or caravans. I adored every second I spent there.

Brett wasn't a jumper like the rest of my social circle, but he quickly realized that it was probably the only way he was ever going to see me. I taught him how to skydive and he picked up the sport quickly. Before long, he began to join me at the weekends on the airfield in Weston, and my circle of friends at the parachute centre welcomed him into our group.

After two years of dating Brett, I decided to take a trip back up to Scotland with him to visit Dad and Frances in Edinburgh. Losing Mum was the hardest thing I had ever had to watch Dad go through, so to see him now, married and happy with life once more, was a relief and I enjoyed spending time with him and Frances. Throughout our stay there, Brett did everything right. He charmed my dad and the pair of them got along well. He took extra care to help out around the house and made a great impression on everyone in the family. *Is everything slotting into place?* I wondered, watching Brett chat away easily to my relatives. *Is he the one I'm supposed to be with?* On paper, he was perfect for me and I loved him.

'Let's go to the castle,' Brett suggested out of the blue one night. We had spent the evening drinking in the city but, glancing at my watch, I knew it was likely to be too late to make it there in time.

'It'll be closed by now,' I replied, shaking my head. 'Can't we just stay here?' It was getting late and I was content to stay at the bar, but Brett seemed on edge.

'No, come on, let's go,' he persisted, desperate for us to head to the castle. 'It doesn't matter if it's closed.'

'What's the point?' I queried, reluctant to leave. 'Will

we even get in?' *Why is he so eager to go to Edinburgh Castle?*

'Of course we will,' Brett quickly replied, finishing his drink before looking at me expectantly. Baffled by his sudden change in mood, I agreed, following him out of the pub, and the two of us began the walk up to the castle. As a member of the military, I knew it would have been relatively easy for us to be let into the battlements after hours, but little did I know that Brett had already arranged it all with the guards on the gate. Everything had been planned perfectly. We arrived at sunset and, without any hassle, we were immediately allowed in to wander aimlessly around. From the top of the castle, we could see the entire city sprawled out below us. It was stunning and I found the walk through the grounds calming. Brett, on the other hand, seemed preoccupied, and I couldn't understand why he had wanted to take me here – until he suddenly stopped and lowered himself down on one knee. I froze, watching him anxiously pull a ring out from his pocket.

'Victoria,' Brett said, his voice shaking slightly as he spoke. 'Will you marry me?' The ring sparkled in his hand as the most spectacular view of the city dimmed in the distance. It was textbook. *I should be over the moon*, I thought to myself, looking down at Brett waiting hopefully. *A dream come true.* But I had a slight sinking feeling that it wasn't quite right. *Do I want to marry Brett?* I asked myself, but before I could figure out an answer I realized a few seconds had passed in silence. *I can't leave him waiting.* I panicked and, having been put on the spot, I had no chance to justify saying anything else.

'Yes,' I answered quietly, allowing Brett to place the engagement ring on my finger. *I'll have time to think about this later*, I resolved, and we celebrated the milestone. I had imagined it would be months, maybe even years, before the wedding would become a reality, but after Brett's proposal life became a whirlwind I couldn't stop.

'There's so much to organize,' he insisted, eager to start the process, and together we began to plan the wedding. Brett wanted the ceremony to take place down south in Sandhurst with an extravagant event, but I just couldn't picture it. I had always hated being the centre of attention, and the idea of walking down the aisle of a packed church with everyone's eyes fixed on me was overwhelmingly daunting. *And besides,* I added to myself, *I want to get married in my hometown.* Every detail that Brett planned for the big day filled me with dread so instead, I turned my focus further towards my parachuting, letting wedding preparations take a back seat. The only thing that seemed to calm the nerves churning away in my stomach was jumping, and so I escaped to the parachute centre, hopping on a lift to leave my problems on the ground.

'Your life's a bit hectic,' Brett commented when another weekend went by with me away at the airfield. 'I hardly ever get to see you.'

'We'll figure it out,' I shrugged, not wanting to deal with the real problem in our relationship. I felt guilty, knowing Brett was longing for me to be more involved in organizing the wedding, but I couldn't tear myself away from skydiving.

'Maybe we should take a break from jumping for a while,' he replied. It was something Brett had suggested on more than one occasion, but each time he did, I refused.

'I can't just halt my training now,' I protested. 'I've come so far with it.' It felt like I was being forced to make a choice between my fiancé and parachuting, and I was scared of what the outcome might be. To add extra pressure, Brett often had to go away for weeks at a time with the army, and so my parents agreed to travel down south for a few days to help out with the wedding plans.

'We've got a lot to go through,' Frances beamed, looking through the list of jobs that needed doing, but I failed to react.

'I suppose,' I replied, distracted by my own thoughts. *Maybe Brett's right*, I considered. *What if I should give up the parachuting?* After all, it was getting in the way of my wedding. *Why isn't this wedding a priority to me?* I wondered, before shaking off the thought. No matter how hard I tried, I just could not bring myself to get excited about the looming day. During their stay, one afternoon Dad and Frances sat me down to lunch.

'Is there anything wrong, Victoria?' Dad asked once the three of us were alone. 'You don't seem yourself.'

'Not at all,' I replied, surprised by the question. 'I'm fine.'

'Are you sure?' he continued with a worried look on his face, not believing me. 'You just don't seem quite as excited about the wedding as we would expect you to be.' I wasn't sure whether it was the mounting pressure or the fact that someone had finally noticed my reluctance to go through with the wedding, but suddenly I burst into tears. If either Dad or Frances were shocked by my response, they didn't show it.

'I don't know if I want to do this,' I admitted, sobbing at the table. 'How do you know if it's the right thing?' Dad took hold of my hand, giving it a squeeze.

'If you've met the right person then you'll know,' he replied softly, glancing from me to Frances. 'If you want to marry Brett, you'll know.'

'Well, I don't know,' I replied, wiping the tears from my eyes.

'Then it's not too late,' Frances chimed in reassuringly. 'It's fixable.'

'She's right,' Dad agreed. 'We'd rather stop things now, a few months before the wedding, than get even closer or make a mistake.' I nodded and instantly relief washed over me. *My dad is right*, I realized, and in my mind, I was set. *I can't marry Brett. I just can't go ahead with it.* I dreaded the awkward conversation we would inevitably have, but I knew the marriage would be doomed from the start. I wanted to spend all of my time jumping while he wanted to focus on the wedding and, in the end,

I knew which one I could live without. Brett was crushed when I broke the news and I felt awful.

'I don't understand,' he answered after a few uncomfortable seconds of silence. 'Are you breaking up with me?'

'No,' I insisted, feeling incredibly guilty. 'I just can't go through with the wedding.'

That evening, we stayed up and discussed it, ultimately deciding to stay together but cancel our plans of marriage. Over the next few weeks, we tried our best to make things work, but calling off the engagement was something our relationship just couldn't recover from and before long, I moved alone from Headley Court to Pirbright, an army training regiment in Surrey. During the last conversation I had with Brett, he mentioned that he had felt my slight hesitation in Edinburgh Castle but had put the thought to the back of his mind. And with the benefit of hindsight, I can see that I loved him like a friend rather than a lover.

*I'm still so young*, I told myself, only in my early twenties. *I have plenty of time to get married.*

I was busy at Pirbright, where I was running a department. About a year after Brett and I had split, I met a man named Liam. He was a troop commander living in the mess I was staying in and, unlike Brett, Liam was already a jumper. Meeting him felt like fate. Instead of getting annoyed at how much time I spent at the parachute centre, Liam understood, and more often than not he spent the weekends jumping alongside me. Living in the same mess meant we could spend all our spare time together and so our relationship became close very quickly. When Liam proposed about a year after we met, it felt right and everything seemed to click into place. I trusted him completely and my family adored him. *I want to go through with this*, I thought to myself. *This time it's different.*

Just before we were due to be married, Liam was abruptly posted to Northern Ireland as a Watchkeeper, which is an operations officer in a Brigade HQ. The post involved the day-to-day running of the ops room and incident control. He worked in shifts, four days and nights on, four off, which meant we had a four-day window to get married in, and no chance of a honeymoon. The thought of a massive wedding still filled me with horror, so we tied the knot in a small ceremony at my home church of Haddington in 2004. The day went by quietly, with only family and close friends in attendance – it was the wedding I had always dreamt of.

After the wedding, I discovered I was also being moved and was posted up to Chilwell, a Reserves Training and Mobilization Centre in Nottingham.

'That's just as well,' Liam responded when I told him the news. 'I think I want to change jobs.' He had decided he wanted to become an ammunition technical officer, meaning he would need to attend bomb disposal training in Kineton. However, the change in careers for Liam also meant he would be away for eighteen months, only returning home to our married quarters at Chilwell at the weekends. *But we're newlyweds*, I thought, horrified at the idea of him leaving for so long, but I didn't want Liam to feel unsupported.

'We'll get through it,' I told him, forcing a smile onto my face.

'Of course we will,' Liam grinned. 'And I'll ring you every evening.'

It seemed straightforward enough and Liam kept to his word, phoning me each night before we went to sleep. For a while we plodded along happily, keeping in touch over the phone or through texts before Liam would return home on Friday evenings. After six months we bought a little house in Oakham, a two-up two-down terrace that was a perfect first home. We tried our best to maintain a normal marriage, but managing a weekend relationship was harder than either of us had imagined and we began to grow distant. During that time, I was also in a local parachuting team with my two best friends, Jude and Sarah. It involved a lot of free flying at the weekends while we trained for British nationals, putting additional stress on the precious time Liam and I had together. Part-way through our first year of marriage, Liam started to act slightly differently. Usually we'd talk for hours on the phone each night and be in touch during the day, but all of that seemed to dwindle.

'I can't make it back this weekend,' he bluntly told me over the phone one day. 'Sorry.'

'That's a shame.' I felt my heart drop. 'How come?'

I didn't want to suspect that he was up to something, but every excuse he could think of came up over the next few weeks and the number of weekends he didn't come home rapidly increased. When Liam did come back, he was very protective of his phone, covering the screen from view. I tried to ignore it but, noticing his change in behaviour, I couldn't help but have a quick look at his phone on the rare occasion he left it unattended. A couple of times I noticed a woman's name – Lucy – pop up, and the messages she sent struck me as odd. *Thinking of the pancakes we made together*, one of the texts read. *I miss looking at the stars with you*, said another. *That sounds a bit intimate*, I noted. Although the messages didn't seem right, Liam wasn't overtly doing anything wrong and he had always been adamant he'd never cheat. *It'll just be the stress*, I told myself, putting the lack of communication between us down to Liam's intense training in bomb disposal. *He needs to be focused.* For his course, there was continuous assessment, and I knew he had already failed a few exams so I set my concerns aside.

We waded our way through the rough patch for a good few months but then, just as quickly as things had gone wrong, everything started to improve. Liam was coming to the end of his course and it was as though I had got my old husband back. We began to have fun together again. *We must be over this blip*, I thought, feeling calmer knowing that soon there'd be less pressure on the relationship. We had started talking about the possibility of starting a family, but I knew that with both of us serving in completely different roles, having children would be near impossible.

'At this rate, we're never going to live together,' I explained. 'If I leave the army, I could join the Ministry of Defence as a physio.'

I knew that if I changed jobs, I'd be able to follow Liam around to wherever he might get posted. The idea of leaving the military made me sad but I had to look to the future. I wanted the freedom to make life choices for myself.

'It's a good idea,' Liam agreed and I beamed, relieved to hear him sound enthusiastic about the plan. I moved over to the MoD in 2007, into essentially the same job but without the uniform or the deployments. We weren't in a rush to have children, but I had thought about it and it felt like a natural progression that was expected of us. *I'm still in my early thirties*, I thought. *I'm not past it yet.* Even so, there was a certain amount of pressure on us, with Liam's parents having mentioned the dreaded biological clock several times, and it was nice to know children were potentially on the horizon now.

One afternoon I returned home from a day of meetings to the landline ringing. *It must be my dad*, I assumed – he was the only person I knew who didn't use a mobile. I reached for the handset that stood on the living room table.

'Hello?' I said, but as soon as I answered the call, the

person on the other end quickly hung up. *That was odd*, I thought, putting the phone back down on the stand. *Perhaps it was a wrong number.* But the phone rang a few more times throughout the day, and with each dropped call I became increasingly confused. The fifth time I picked up the phone, a woman spoke on the other end.

'Hi, sorry to disturb you.' She spoke with a Canadian accent. 'I just wanted to phone you to tell you what an amazing husband you have.'

'Um . . .' I hesitated, the woman's remark catching me off guard. 'OK.'

'I'm on a course with him,' she added.

'Right.' I didn't know what to say. My mind raced, trying to think if Liam had mentioned any of the women on his course.

'I think you're really lucky to have him,' the woman continued as I listened in disbelief. 'He really loves you and I just thought it would be nice for you to know that.' Alarm bells started to ring. *This is all a bit strange*, I thought to myself, but I didn't respond. Instead I listened while she gushed about how amazing Liam was, waiting until she went quiet.

'What's your name?' I eventually queried.

'Lucy,' the woman answered. *Lucy?* I recognized that name but I couldn't quite place it, until suddenly the penny dropped. She was the woman he had been messaging. My jaw fell, with a sick feeling creeping into my stomach.

'Are you having an affair with my husband?' I blurted out.

'Oh no, no,' Lucy insisted. 'Nothing like that.' But I didn't believe her.

'Something is going on,' I continued. 'I've seen your messages.'

'It's nothing,' Lucy tried to reply, but I refused to accept her excuses and eventually she broke down. 'Well, yes, but it's finished now.' I gulped, dreading what I was about to find out.

'How long has it been going on for?' I felt my voice quivering but I willed myself not to get upset.

'Just under a year,' Lucy admitted, and I nearly dropped the phone.

'A year?' I was stunned. Overwhelmed, I wanted to cry but I persevered. *I need to get as much information as I can out of her.*

'It was after a party.' Lucy tried to answer my questions but I couldn't take any more. I hung up the phone and stood frozen to the spot in the living room. *What do I do?* I thought to myself. I considered packing up the house, tearing down every photo I had of us, but ultimately there was only one thing I could do. The dial tone rang twice before Liam answered.

'You need to get back here right now,' I told him.

'I've been on duty, I can't—' Liam broke off, noticing the harsh tone of my voice. 'Is something wrong?'

'I don't care if you've been on duty.' I felt like I could burst into tears at any second but I kept my voice blunt.

'If you want this marriage then you come back here now.' Before he could answer, I turned off the phone. *If he doesn't come back, that's the end of it*, I told myself, but before long I heard Liam's car pull up on the driveway.

'What's the matter?' His voice sounded panicked as he rushed through the door, and as soon as I told him what had happened, he broke down in tears.

'How could you do this to me?' I asked, at a loss for how I should react.

'I'm really, really sorry,' Liam begged. 'I didn't mean to.'

'I want to know everything now,' I snapped back, needing to hear the truth from him. I listened in silence as he told me they had been friends at first.

'There was a function at the mess, you know, where everyone's drinking and stuff,' Liam started to explain. 'I'd gone up to bed and she followed me into the room and got into bed beside me, that's how it started.' Heartbroken, I couldn't listen any more.

'I'm going to the toilet,' I said, getting up.

'I ended it, Vicky,' Liam called after me. 'I chose you.' Ignoring him as I left the room, I slyly slipped his phone into my pocket while I headed up the stairs. It was the days before thumbprints and password-protected phones, and as I clicked the lock on the bathroom door into place, I dialled Lucy's number.

'Hey!' she exclaimed, clearly thinking it was Liam calling. I felt my anger froth over.

'You bitch,' I snapped and, unable to stop myself, I laid into her. 'You think you can just destroy my marriage.' It was as though I had switched into autopilot and once I had started, I couldn't stop, calling her every name under the sun until she started to cry.

'How can you just try to ruin my marriage like that?' I went on. I knew all too well that it takes two to tango, but I was dealing with her at this point. 'How dare you go into his room.'

Liam was still downstairs but hearing me shout, he sprinted up to the bathroom and began banging on the door.

'Let me in, Vicky,' he called out, before twisting the lock from the outside to get into the room, prising the phone from my grip. I crumpled to the floor, totally distraught by what Liam had done. He sat down beside me and told me everything. Lucy was a Canadian officer who had come over to do the bomb disposal training. A small part of me wanted to write to her commanding officer. *Infidelity is really frowned upon in the military*, I thought to myself. *I could tell her CO exactly what she did.*

I never did write that letter, but having the small power of knowing I could helped me get through the first few weeks afterwards. I tried to get over what Liam had done but I couldn't forgive him. The trust was gone and that was what I struggled with the most. *I trusted him implicitly*, I battled internally. *And yet he betrayed me.* The friends and family I confided in were stunned by the news, agreeing that Liam just 'wasn't the type' to have an affair. But reality said otherwise.

Not wanting to give up on the marriage entirely, we both moved to Colchester where one of my friends was running a rehab unit.

'I'll see if I can get a job there,' I told Liam, determined that we needed to be under one roof to make our relationship work. As luck would have it, a physio position opened up and I started work there not long after the move. It was my last-ditch attempt to save our marriage, but we hadn't lived in Colchester long when, in 2008, the conflict in Afghanistan intensified and became deeply unpleasant. I knew it was only a matter of time before the inevitable happened.

'They're posting me out there,' Liam confirmed one day. The prospect of him being sent to Afghanistan was hell on earth, and once he was gone I could barely sleep knowing just how stressful and traumatic his environment must have been. I knew he was apprehensive, but it was what they had been training to do. It was always going to happen.

He was abroad for several months at a time, exercising his bomb disposal training whilst the Taliban tried to kill him at every turn. *It must be horrific out there*, I worried, struggling to deal with it at home. In the back of my mind, another fear crept into my thoughts. *What if he cheats on me again?* I tried to brush off the doubts. Afghanistan was hardly the place you went to make relationships.

When Liam returned home, I tried not to let my concerns get the better of me, but I couldn't help but notice how secretive he was over his phone again. When his screen lit up with a message one day, he was quick to turn it off, but not before I caught the Facebook logo and a woman's name, Emma. *It's nothing*, I thought. *Ignore it.*

'It's good to have you back,' I told him, exchanging a small smile before Liam left the room. Just then, his phone flashed up again with another message from Emma. *Is something going on?* I wanted to be understanding about Liam's situation. Being posted out to war was horrific. *It's only natural to form close friendships out there*, I told myself. I knew from my own experience in Kosovo that having people who were going through the same thing made adjusting back home easier, but nonetheless I still didn't trust that Liam wasn't up to something.

On one particular evening, I had ventured on a rare night out with parachuting friends and, having just left a curry house, I bumped into Mel, a woman I knew from the military.

'How are you doing?' I asked, exchanging pleasantries before turning to head home, but she called me back.

'Oh, Vicky,' she added nonchalantly. 'I bumped into your husband in London the other day.'

'Oh?' I answered. *He never told me that he'd seen her in London.*

'I was out with Emma so we all went for drinks,' Mel

continued, with no idea she was saying anything she shouldn't. 'Tell him I said hi.'

'I will do.' I waved goodbye, heading away from the conversation. I wanted to confront him about Emma, but Liam was going back to Afghanistan soon and I didn't want to distract him or put extra strain on him when he would be in such a dangerous situation. Instead I returned my focus to my work at Netheravon Parachute Centre. I wanted to become an accelerated free-fall instructor, so I spent the weekends travelling from Colchester to Netheravon. While Liam was gone, the familiar torment of not really knowing where he was or who he was with sank back in. *I can't live like this*, I realized. My nerves were driving me crazy. What I really wanted was a job closer to Netheravon so I didn't need to travel as far to do jumps and, spotting a job at Larkhill, I felt torn about what to do. *Liam would happily move with me*, I noted, knowing that if I waited until he came back from tour, we could move properly. *But that's not what I want*. Making up my mind, I decided to do something that I still feel guilty about today. I didn't really fully discuss the move with Liam and instead, I transferred to Larkhill on my own while he was away.

'At least there are no children involved,' said all those who found out about our separation. While they may have been right, it was still unbearably sad that our marriage was ending. I had assumed I was going to be with Liam for life.

\* \* \*

I threw myself into my parachuting training, spending more time than ever at the airfield. The first time I attempted the instructor course, I failed on one of the jumps and so I had to repeat it.

'Will you do some filming for this jump, Vicky?' another member of staff asked me one weekend.

'No problem,' I agreed. The filming meant jumping with a team, recording them on a camera as they fell. I was responsible for recording the display with someone else filming from further away, spinning through the air in a wider, faster circle behind me. I think he must have misjudged one of the turns, because all of a sudden he collided with me and the metal smoke canister on his ankle struck both the side of my arm and the side of my helmet, denting the metal plate. I don't think the cameraman had realized how badly he had hit me. When you're falling at a speed of 170 miles per hour, even just the slightest blow can come with an extreme force. *Something's wrong with my wrist*, I realized, not allowing the panic to set in. *I need to get down safely.* I pulled on the parachute, but I couldn't use my wrist properly. With the usual fast descent no longer an option, and no chance of hitting the small landing spot in front of the crowd, I steered myself gently to a big, open area where I was able to touch down safely.

I felt a bit rough after that. It was a fractured wrist, leaving me relieved that I wasn't more seriously injured. However, the incident had happened just a few weeks before I had to do my second accelerated free-fall course.

*I've already paid for it*, I thought, and I knew I had already put too much time and effort into it to give up now. I was determined to do this course no matter what, so I decided to simply strap up my broken wrist before boarding the aircraft. But moments before the jump was due to take place, I received a phone call from another bomb disposal soldier in Afghanistan with Liam.

'Just in case you hear anything on the grape-vine,' the soldier on the other end told me, 'there's been an ATO killed, blown up in Afghan, and I just wanted to let you know that it's not Liam.' It was army protocol that if someone was killed on tour there was immediate radio silence so that people couldn't communicate in or out. The point of it was to stop Chinese whispers and similar incidents going on, but information still manages to get in and out.

'OK, thanks.' I was just about to do a jump, but it was hard to focus knowing that Liam was out there risking his life. *Should I really be here?* Regardless of what state our marriage was in by now, the worry was still unbelievably difficult to deal with. Liam was OK, but unfortunately someone else wasn't.

I passed the course and in 2009 I finally achieved my goal of becoming a qualified accelerated free-fall instructor. When Liam came home I did try to persuade him that we should give our marriage another chance. I panicked at the thought of that being it, the end of the story, but he didn't agree and I had to let it go. We separated but have always remained on friendly terms.

On my own now, I bought a house in Bulford, not far from Larkhill, and life continued. Every weekend I worked as an instructor at Netheravon, which was quite tough during the summer, as I was working seven days a week. As an AFF instructor I could train up people who had never had any exposure to skydiving over a six-hour ground school, then introduce them to the air. The first three jumps were with two instructors, then if the student was deemed capable the next four jumps were with one instructor. Once these seven levels had been completed, the student did a low-level solo jump and ten consolidation jumps. Part of the reason behind juggling my two jobs was to try and cover my mortgage, but more than that, the parachute centre was still very much my social life. Outside of that, I didn't really have anything – I had hardly any friends who weren't involved in either the army or parachuting. I thought that I would be married and planning a family at this stage and instead I was single again. My life was very busy but at times it felt empty too.

It was the winter of 2009 when I first met Emile. He walked into my treatment room at Larkhill and I realized that I had seen him around a few times at the regiment's gym.

'Emile, is it?' I asked, looking through his notes, and he nodded. He was a unit PTI (physical training instructor) in the Royal Artillery who had injured his knee badly on a skiing trip, resulting in quite extensive reconstructive surgery. Just from looking at his knee, I knew it would be a long time before he'd be able to walk properly or do anything physical.

'I need to get better because I'm joining the Physical Training Corps,' Emile told me, seeming quite low. *I need to figure out what makes him tick*, I thought to myself. Part of my job was to develop a rapport with my patients by tapping into their interests. It had always been a fool-proof way to get them on side, in order to help get them back up to fitness.

'You won't be joining physical training any time soon at this rate,' I admitted. 'But if you take your physio seriously, it's an achievable goal.'

Again, Emile nodded, his eyes almost glazed over. I could see that, while he was listening, none of the information I was offering to him was going in. He'd lost interest. *I need to make him care about rehabilitation*, I thought to myself, and so I started talking.

'You injured yourself skiing, is that right?' I asked, sitting down beside him.

'That's right,' Emile replied, shifting in his seat.

'It's quite an adventurous sport,' I commented. 'It must be similar to skydiving, I imagine.'

'How so?' Emile's tone seemed almost sarcastic.

'That feeling of flying,' I continued, purposefully likening my love of parachuting to skiing. 'It's like freedom.'

'I've never been skydiving,' Emile jumped into the conversation, and I began to tell him all about the parachute centre.

*It's working*. I beamed, pleased to have got him talking. Emile was a reluctant patient, but over the next few weeks I managed to cultivate a good working relationship with him, and he started coming in regularly for physio. Initially, there wasn't much of an attraction there – we just became genuinely good friends. But over time, Emile grew on me and, after a few months, there was an evident spark between us. I couldn't help but notice his eyes – they were a piercing blue – but I had always tended to be more attracted to people's personalities. The way someone is, what drives them, is what has always been important to me, and I like someone who possesses ambition and passion. I saw the way Emile cared about his career, intensely rehabbing himself because he wanted to join the Physical Training Corps, and I admired him for it. Everything he did, he wanted to do well, especially sports. He was in shape and motivated to stay that way. He knew where he wanted to go in life and made it happen. Emile didn't just sit around and talk about ideas that he'd never actually follow up, he made sure he achieved his goals.

'I've got two children,' Emile told me one day in conversation, explaining they were from his previous marriage. 'They're my entire world.' I liked how readily he volunteered details about his life.

'Are you still married?' I asked. *I could do without a complicated relationship*, I thought, still hurt from the way my marriage to Liam had ended.

'I'm married on paper but we're separated,' Emile told

me. At first, I was unsure. *I've been here before*, I thought to myself, keen to avoid another unfaithful relationship, but when I discovered Emile was living in the mess rather than at home, I realized he was telling the truth. When he sent me a Facebook message asking me out for a drink, I transferred his care over to my colleague and shortly after, we started dating.

For our first date he took me to Wales climbing and to do an aerial assault course. The day in the treetops was windy and I remember us both standing on the plat-form up in the trees, swaying with the wind and grinning at each other. He had an energy and enthusiasm for new experiences. He loved outdoor sports and activities, and it was great to have someone in my life again who'd share these interests with me. His choice of date in Wales had set the bar high, so for my turn we went coasteering in Devon. As we jumped off some rocks into the sea, I realized firstly that I was freezing and secondly that this was not my thing at all! Luckily, unlike me Emile was a strong swimmer, so although I was truly out of my com-fort zone I felt safe enough with him.

He would come over to my house in Bulford in the evenings and we would spend many hours drinking wine and talking long into the night. About our lives, what made us tick and what we wanted for the future. We just seemed to 'click'.

# 3

# Emile

The beginning of the new relationship was a whirlwind. Emile was like no one I had met before and he utterly charmed me. Even though we'd only known each other for a few weeks, we were inseparable and I was eager to learn all about his past. He told me that he was originally from Cape Town in South Africa, having come to the UK as an adult.

'I had only come over for a bit of work experience,' he explained to me one night. 'I just wanted to spend some time in another country before returning to South Africa.' He had taken me out for evening drinks and, as we sat by the bar, he told me about the months he had spent settling into life in the UK, working in bars and restaurants.

'Why did you end up staying?' I asked. The idea of growing up in South Africa sounded incredible, and I couldn't imagine why he would swap that exotic life for grey and rainy England.

'It was because of my kids,' he explained, before going into the details of his marriage. 'I met Carly when I came over to England, before I joined the army, but we had only been seeing each other for about four months when she fell pregnant.'

'Really?' I replied between sips of my wine. 'That must have been quite a shock.'

'It was,' Emile agreed, nodding at me. 'I didn't know what to think at first, because it wasn't a serious relationship and I didn't particularly want to stay with her. But at the same time, I didn't want to go back to South Africa while having a child over here in the UK. That didn't seem right.'

'That sounds reasonable,' I answered, respecting his decision. I liked the fact that Emile had stuck by his kids.

'Carly and I decided to just have a registry office wedding,' he continued, pausing to take a swig from his pint. 'So that I would be able to stay here.'

'I see,' I replied, liking Emile more with each thing I heard about him.

'It was just one of those things,' he went on. 'I never really loved her. The only reason I married her was because it made it easier for me to see our child. I just wanted to do the right thing.' It was apparent there was no love lost between Emile and his ex-wife, and I listened as he continued to speak poorly of her. 'She stopped working when she got pregnant and it got to the point where my daughter was about four. I suggested that she should go back to work, but she decided to get pregnant again instead.'

He said he felt duty-bound to have another child with

Carly, to give his daughter a brother or sister. *His attitude towards his ex is rather bad*, I thought to myself, feeling slightly uncomfortable as I listened to him condemn her as being lazy and work-shy. Alarm bells should have started to ring in my head, but I dismissed it. *I have no reason not to believe it's true*, I decided. *For all I know, she trapped him by getting pregnant.*

My relationship with Emile was moving rapidly. He was incredibly intense right from the off, wanting to spend every second he could with me and, while it did all feel a little bit too soon, I couldn't help but enjoy the attention he showered me with. We worked in the same building, and he was always making excuses to pop in to see me throughout the day, sometimes even bringing a coffee over for me. We spent most of our spare time together too. Emile would make the effort to help me out around the house and I felt like the centre of his world. He was so passionate that I got swept up by it all.

'I love you,' he told me for the first time after only a few weeks of dating, and upon hearing this confession I blushed.

'I love you too,' I admitted. He was the complete opposite of Liam, who had been distant and busy with work most of the time, especially towards the end of our marriage. On the flip side, Emile cancelled his other plans so that he could spend more time with me. *I've never had so much attention before*, I realized, and it felt nice to be made a priority. After a few months of seeing each other, Emile moved into my house. It felt like a natural progression – after all, he spent most nights at mine anyway.

'I'm going to ask Carly if the kids can come round,' Emile announced to me one day.

'Oh, sure,' I replied. It niggled me slightly that he hadn't asked me or seemed to consider whether I was ready to meet his children. *This is a big step*, I thought, worried that Emile may be moving things along too soon. However, I decided against voicing my concerns – I was hardly going to stop him from bringing his children over.

'I want to see the children on a more regular basis,' he told Carly over the phone as I sat beside him. He was blunt with her and I could sense things hadn't ended on great terms. Understandably, Carly told Emile that she wanted to meet me first before letting the kids stay with us.

'That's fine,' I told him when he relayed her answer back to me. 'I'll happily meet her for a coffee.'

'Really?' Emile replied, a smile spreading across his face. 'That would be great.' He sent Carly a text and, just like that, a date was set.

Meeting his ex-wife went as well as it could have done. I had been so nervous, knowing how much it meant to Emile, but now sitting across from Carly in a local coffee shop, we were getting along fine. We didn't really talk about Emile, but she asked a lot of questions about me and my life. In hindsight, and having children of my own now, I fully understand her need to know about me.

'I'll sort it out then with Emile, and figure out when the kids can come round,' Carly told me, finishing her latte.

'That's brilliant, he'll be thrilled,' I enthused. 'And it would be nice to meet the kids.' Carly smiled, picking her coat up from the back of her chair.

'It was good to meet you, Vicky,' she said, throwing the coat over her shoulders.

'And it was great to meet you,' I replied, relieved that the meeting had gone so well. As Carly began to head to the door, she paused, turning back to me.

'Of course, well . . .' She hesitated before dropping the bombshell. 'I assume you know about the other children.'

'What other children?' I asked, confused by what she was implying.

'Oh, maybe it's for Emile to tell you,' Carly answered in haste, turning back around to leave.

'No,' I stopped her. 'You've told me now, you need to tell me the rest.' I felt sick, fearing whatever secret she had.

'Well, Emile had a girlfriend back in South Africa,' Carly explained to me uncomfortably. 'They'd had a couple of children there, but she and the kids live in the UK now.' I was floored by what I was hearing. *Is this true?* I asked myself. *How could Emile have not brought this up?*

'I see,' I nodded, not wanting to show how upset the news was making me. Honestly, however, I didn't know what to think, and I mulled it over as I drove home. *We agreed to be honest with one another, and when we discussed our pasts he chose not to tell me.* The idea that he had been deliberately hiding this from me was almost too much to bear. But even so, I wanted to believe he would have his reasons.

*Am I being oversensitive?* I wondered. I didn't want the issues over secrets in my previous relationship to creep into this one. *He could have been planning to tell me.* When I got home I immediately confronted Emile, who jumped up from his spot on the couch.

'I didn't know how to mention it,' he started to explain, his voice trembling slightly.

'You should have told me,' I snapped, hurt by the lie.

'I wanted to.' Emile looked as though he was going to cry. 'But I wasn't sure how to bring it up.'

'I don't know if I can stay in a relationship where you're not being honest,' I admitted, pacing the living room anxiously. 'I've just left one deceitful marriage.'

'I was going to tell you,' he insisted. 'I was always going to tell you.'

'That's not the point though,' I replied, my tone softening. 'You should have told me sooner.' I could tell Emile was upset.

'I'm so sorry,' he pleaded. 'I don't want to lose you.'

I didn't know what to make of it, but I decided to believe him. *It would have hardly stayed a secret for long*, I resolved. *I would have met his parents at some point and the cat would have been out of the bag.*

'Why would you keep this from me?' I asked, trying to understand him.

'I don't have anything to do with them,' Emile replied. 'That's why I haven't brought them up with you yet.'

'But they live in the UK?' I asked, thinking back to the scraps of information I had got from Carly.

'Yes, they do,' he confirmed, before adding, 'it was the mother's choice to keep them from me, not mine. She doesn't let me have any contact with them.'

'OK,' I replied, choosing to let the issue go. 'But we have to be honest with each other from now on.'

Emile agreed and, after that conversation, we put it aside. From then on, Emile's eldest two children were never really mentioned again. *Is this another warning sign?* I stressed to myself. Emile had walked away from two of his children, and the idea that he could so easily forget about them felt alien to me. But he didn't have any contact with them at all, and it seemed as though the thought of them was painful for him, so it was put to one side. And he seemed to have a good relationship with Carly's kids, who were quite young at the time.

Meanwhile, the pair of us had discussed the possibility of having children of our own. By now I was in my mid-thirties, and the biological clock I had been warned about was ticking in my mind.

'I don't want to enter a long-term relationship where there is no possibility of having children,' I explained to

Emile. I was quite up front about where I stood on that from the start.

'No, I know,' he replied, agreeing with my thoughts for the future. 'I'd love to have children with you.' Hearing the excitement in Emile's voice, I smiled. I wasn't sure if I was just selectively ignoring what had gone on in his past because of what I wanted, but I was so utterly head-over-heels in love with Emile, and that made it difficult to take a step back and view the bigger picture. *He wants to have a baby with me*, I thought, excited about what the future could look like. Emile's affection was as intense as ever and it was a nice feeling to be the object of someone's desire. He was cooking meals for me after work, having my favourite bottle of wine waiting for me in the fridge when I arrived home, and I was too happy in my relationship to worry about the issues from his past.

*I love you so much, have a great day*, said a Post-it note on a cupboard door in the kitchen. I grinned, opening the door to find another note inside. *Still love you!* it read. They were just soppy little thoughts he had scribbled on paper, but the notes were a constant reminder that Emile's attention was always on me.

After the misery of a weekend marriage with Liam, barely seeing him and dealing with his distant behaviour, the bombardment of passion I received from Emile was a new experience for me. It felt nice to have someone focused on me. *Emile is a good man*, I thought to myself. *He's made mistakes, but it was his exes' faults as much as it was his*. I decided that I had to take Emile at face value. I knew the man he was now was caring and family centred, so his previous relationships didn't matter to me.

Emile and I shared the same hopes and dreams for the future, and he was more than happy to help me fix up my house. Just before meeting him I had bought quite an old property that needed bits and pieces doing to it every so often. The majority of my DIY had been fairly disastrous.

'Have you stuck this together with black tape?' Emile asked, a slight smirk on his face as he inspected a bookshelf.

'Yes,' I laughed, watching him hold up the botched shelf. 'I'm not very good with this stuff.'

'That's why you've got me,' he replied, ripping the tape down. 'I'll fix it for you.' After that, Emile helped out a lot around the house, busying himself with the odd jobs that needed doing. We seemed like the perfect pair. However, while Emile was helping me with household problems, money had become an apparent issue for him. Not long after he moved in, only a month or so, he began to tell me more and more about his financial situation. I had known Emile had some debts when I met him, but at the time it wasn't something he had wanted to discuss.

'They're mainly because of my ex-wife,' he finally confided in me one evening. 'She stopped working and instead she would just sit at home all day spending money from the joint account.'

'I see,' I replied, taking it in. This new information felt like another bombshell, but at the same time he was so embarrassed telling me about his debts that I felt for him, and I could see how much he wanted to get on top of his finances.

'I'm trying to get it sorted but it's taking time,' he added.

'How much do you owe?' I asked. I didn't want to start a life together in debt.

'About two thousand pounds,' he told me, and I nodded, relieved it wasn't as bad as I had thought it could be.

'I'll clear it for you and you can pay me back,' I offered. I could immediately see the relief on Emile's face. *We'll sort this out together*, I decided. While I waited for Emile to get back on his feet, I taught him how to pack parachutes at the airfield. Picking up the skill quickly, Emile was a natural at it and after that, he would tag along with me to the parachute centre to pack our parachutes for money. With this extra income, Emile made the £2,000 back quite quickly and, with his debt finally cleared, we made the decision to get a joint account.

'It would make sense for household expenses,' I suggested pragmatically. I had opened a joint account with Liam, with both of us paying in each month to cover our bills, and it had worked well.

'Sounds like a good plan,' Emile replied. Everything seemed to be fitting into place.

\* \* \*

I was keen to meet Emile's family and get to know his friends and so, in January 2011, just over a year since we first met, we flew out to South Africa to stay with his parents for three weeks. It was exciting to see where Emile came from and I was welcomed into the family with open arms. His parents were warm and friendly and couldn't do enough to make our stay enjoyable and memorable.

'You know, Emile has never talked about anyone the way he talks about you,' his mother gushed one morning. It was just the two of us sitting together at the breakfast table.

'Really?' I asked, chuffed that he had talked so much about me to them.

'Really,' Emile's mum continued, an excited grin plastered across her face. 'He's never told us that he loves someone before he met you, but he really does love you.'

My cheeks went red but I was ecstatic at what I was hearing. There was a photograph of Carly and her children in their bedroom and they talked a little about her, but never in a negative way. They believed that she and Emile were simply not right for each other.

'Morning,' Emile said, joining us in the kitchen. 'Shall we climb Table Mountain today, Vicky?'

Table Mountain was a massive landmark in Cape Town and, at over 3,500 feet, it was no mean feat to climb. 'It'll take a few hours but we'll have fun,' Emile promised, and so off we went. Being a strong athlete, Emile was a keen rock climber and had given me some training on a local climbing wall, but nothing could have prepared me for

Table Mountain. Emile showed me how to anchor myself to the rock, doing what he called a multi-pitch climb as we clambered up the mountain. He had made an excellent recovery from his injury and, although it occasionally gave him some pain, he had worked hard at rehab and reaped the benefits. So while he was perfectly comfortable with the climb, after several hours I was exhausted and my sense of humour was starting to fail.

'How long left?' I asked through gritted teeth. It was so hot my face felt raw. A lot of the trek had been quite daunting, and we were extremely exposed to the burning sun most of the time. *I'm fed up with this now*, I thought to myself.

'We're nearly at the top,' Emile shouted back at me, navigating us up the mountain, and I grimaced.

'You keep saying that,' I snapped back, feeling like we had been climbing for an eternity. But this time he was right, and as I pulled myself over the edge, Emile helped me to steady myself on my feet.

'Are you all right?' he asked, once we were safely on top of the mountain.

'I'm fine,' I replied quietly. 'It was tougher than I'd thought it would be.'

'Ah.' Emile paused. It was as though he wanted to say something but he seemed to decide against it. We spent a while admiring the view but I couldn't wait to be back on the ground. 'Let's get the cable car back down,' Emile suggested, sensing the slight tension, and I breathed a sigh of relief.

'That would be good,' I replied.

Despite the minor blip of Table Mountain we were having an incredible time and, a few days later, we found ourselves at a cheetah sanctuary. The cheetahs had been rescued after being shot by local farmers, and we were allowed into an enclosure to interact with one of them.

'They're so docile,' I marvelled, carefully petting the big cat.

'They are,' one of the keepers agreed. 'Ask away if you have any questions.' The cheetahs were tame but still had a minder with each of them whilst we were in close proximity, with another member of staff keeping an eye on us from afar. I gave the one near us another stroke.

'Aren't you gorgeous,' I cooed as Emile asked about the animals.

'They tend to hunt cows and sheep from the local farms, which ends up with the farmers shooting the cheetahs, so here we rehabilitate them,' she explained. 'They'll get shot but the bullet probably won't kill them, which is unpleasant for everyone, so we try to help.'

'The cats look like they're doing great,' Emile replied, giving the cheetah a ruffle on the top of his head. 'What do you think?' he asked me.

'They're lovely,' I answered, captivated by how beautiful the creatures were.

'Have you got any more questions?' the minder asked after a few minutes, raising her eyebrows as she smiled at me.

'Yes actually, I've got a question.' Emile turned around to face me, taking my hand. 'Will you marry me?'

I was stunned. The staff must have been in on the surprise because there was a diamond ring on the cheetah's collar. Taking it off, Emile dropped to one knee.

'Yes,' I burst out immediately, a smile spreading across my face. 'Of course I will.' I couldn't believe it – I had to fight to choke back the tears. I hadn't seen it coming but it felt like a dream come true. I was finally getting the happily-ever-after dream I had always had. After my marriage to Liam had ended, I had mourned the loss of a future and come to terms with the fact that children may not factor in my life. Now all that had changed. This time, the proposal felt right. *This is meant to be*, I thought. Emile grinned, standing up to fit the ring onto my finger as the sanctuary staff applauded. I blushed, slightly embarrassed by the public display. It was the opposite of what I would have normally wanted but the proposal felt perfect all the same. It had all happened so fast, but I was ready to settle down, and when the commotion of our engagement died down – all the messages on social media and texts congratulating us were overwhelming to start with – Emile and I decided we would get married in South Africa.

'My parents won't be able to afford flights to England,' he explained to me, and I understood.

'Let me speak to my dad first,' I replied, but one quick phone call later and the decision for a destination wedding felt like a no-brainer.

'Frances and I would be delighted to come to wherever you plan your wedding,' Dad said, on board with the idea straight away. 'I'll support you no matter what.'

'Amazing, thanks so much, Dad,' I replied, knowing I could count on him. Putting the phone down, I had never felt luckier. 'Wedding in South Africa it is,' I announced to Emile, and we spent the rest of our holiday looking at venues for September that year.

A few months before our big day, I realized I was late for my period.

'I'll just do a test to check,' I told Emile, fully expecting it to be negative. When I later held the stick in my hands, I burst out with, 'Oh my god.'

'What?' Emile gasped as he stood beside me, taking the stick into his own hands. 'You're pregnant?'

'I can't believe it.' I stared at the pregnancy test, almost anticipating that the result would change, but every time I blinked the two lines remained the same.

'That's great!' Emile cheered, throwing his arms around me. 'Are you happy?'

'I am,' I replied, still in shock, but as I thought about the idea of a little baby to welcome home, I beamed. 'I can't wait.'

In the ideal world I had envisioned, we would have been married for a few years before we started a family, but by now I was thirty-six. *Better sooner rather than later*, I decided, excited at the prospect of becoming a mum. The next few weeks carried on as normal, with the occasional trip to the shops to look at baby clothes.

'We might be able to find some baby stuff when we go to London,' I commented, wandering down the baby aisle. Emile was due to play in a cricket match in London but because he would need to stay overnight, we had decided to make a trip out of it, with a night out planned in the city for after the match.

'Definitely,' Emile agreed. 'We'll have a look round when we get there.' I couldn't imagine anything would go wrong, but by the time match day rolled around, I noticed I had started to bleed.

'Something's not right,' I panicked, and Emile rushed us to hospital. I lay down on the table, watching as the sonographer searched the screen. I waited anxiously for a heartbeat but the room remained silent. Eventually, a doctor arrived to confirm what we already knew.

'I'm so sorry, we can't find a heartbeat,' the consultant broke the news. 'You've miscarried the baby.'

I was twelve weeks pregnant and, sadly, it was more common than I had realized. *I just never thought it would be me.*

'It's entirely up to you what we do now,' the doctor continued. 'You can either be admitted into hospital and have a removal, or you can elect to let nature take its course.'

'I guess I'll let nature do its thing,' I said without another thought, longing to be back at home. The doctor nodded.

'Let's get you home then,' he replied.

Emile drove us back to the house and, while at first he seemed gutted about the loss, his mind was preoccupied by the cricket.

'I just don't know whether we should go or not,' he voiced, glancing at me in the passenger seat. 'Would you feel up to it?'

'Um . . .' I paused, not knowing what to say. *I don't want to travel to London*, I thought. The journey alone would take over an hour, and the idea of having to socialize at a time like this felt like hell. 'What do you want to do?'

'I don't know.' Emile stared at the road ahead. 'I don't want to let anyone down.'

'Do you want to go?' I asked him, knowing he did, and Emile shrugged.

'They've already booked our accommodation,' he answered, and I quietly sighed.

'Well, we can't save the baby,' I started, trying to think it through logically. 'The baby's gone, it's not going to happen.' I paused, hoping Emile would interject, but he didn't. 'So whatever we do is not going to make any difference.'

'Right,' he replied, giving me a small smile. 'Maybe we should go then.' *I guess that's the plan.* I felt like I could easily cry but I had no choice but to go along with it.

The drive to London was slow, and the further away from home we got, the worse the pain became.

'Once we're in the hotel room, it won't be so bad,' Emile promised, noticing my discomfort.

'Hopefully,' I replied, subtly clutching my stomach for dear life. I closed my eyes, wishing the whole way the journey would end until, blissfully, I finally heard Emile turn off the engine. We were staying in the centre of London, but as soon as we were inside the building, I realized they hadn't put us up in a hotel.

'Here's the team's room,' a staff member said, showing us to the large, empty room.

'There's no beds?' I asked, and the mess employee shook his head.

'No, not for this room.' He pointed at the sleeping bags and roll mats piled up in the corner. I looked around for any sign of a bathroom, but there was just the communal one several flights of stairs below us.

'Emile.' I stared at the empty space. 'I don't want to be here.' Another wave of pain hit me as my stomach cramped. *Let's go home*, I thought. *This was a mistake.*

'But we're already here now, Vicky,' Emile protested. 'I can't just leave them.'

'I can't sleep in this room.' I was already losing a lot of blood and the thought of anyone noticing would have been humiliating.

'Do you want to just take the keys then?' he asked, offering the car keys to me.

'Oh,' I muttered.

*Tell the team you're leaving*, I pleaded internally. *Tell them your fiancée is having a miscarriage.* I wanted to convince him to come with me, but I was experiencing what felt like the world's worst period pains and I urgently needed to leave. 'Good luck with your game,' I told him, taking the car keys.

The drive back home took what felt like an eternity. One hand on the wheel, the other hand pressed against my tummy, I fixated on the road stretched out in front of me. *He's going on a night out in London,* I thought, *instead of taking care of me.* It felt completely out of character for Emile, since he had always been so attentive. *It's partly my fault*, I rationalized. *I did tell him he could go.* Whilst I was returning home, he called a friend to come and stay with me so I didn't have to be alone, although the only person I wanted there, the only person who should have been there, was nowhere to be seen. I didn't really know what to feel. Along with the anger I felt towards Emile for leaving me to deal with this on my own was a gut-wrenching disappointment that he just didn't seem to understand how it felt to be losing your baby.

After the way Emile had initially dealt with the miscarriage, I decided not to take any time off from work. *I'm just going to get on with life.* The only way I knew how to cope was to keep busy, block it out and carry on. *It wasn't meant to be*, I told myself and refused to wallow. Oddly enough, Emile seemed to have a bit of a delayed reaction to the miscarriage and, while I was determined to keep going, he was quite low for a couple of weeks. He seemed to resent the fact that I'd gone back to work and wanted me to be at home with him.

Six weeks later, the day we were due to fly to South Africa for the wedding, I realized I was a couple of days late for my period again. I immediately took another test. Once again, those small but significant double lines appeared.

'We're having a baby,' I announced to Emile, squealing with excitement.

'That's amazing,' Emile grinned. We were over the moon. In a way, it made the trip back to Emile's hometown even more special, to be taking our little baby along with us. While Emile had been through pregnancy before, it felt like the first time for both of us. He was so excited and interested in all the minute details. He downloaded an app that told us day by day how the baby was developing, and each day he'd fill me in on our baby's progress.

The day of the wedding was the stuff of fantasy. The ceremony was at Camps Bay, overlooking the sea. As I walked down the aisle alongside my dad, I couldn't believe this was reality. I imagined the baby, cosy in my tummy, the baby I had always wanted, and as I walked towards Emile I didn't think life could get any more perfect. Almost two years after we had first started dating and nine months after the engagement, Emile and I were married.

After the wedding, we flew back to London for one night before taking the train to Paris for our honeymoon. It was a dreamy few days, meandering around the tourist traps and heading to Disneyland for a couple of nights. But one evening at the theme park, while we were queuing outside a restaurant, I suddenly felt a horrible rushing sensation, like I was going to wet myself.

'I need to go to the bathroom,' I quickly told Emile, hurrying inside to use the restaurant toilets. Once I was in the stall, I pulled my pants down to find blood. *Oh.* I sat down in defeat. *I'm losing another baby.*

I walked back out, holding on to my stomach as it started to cramp. It felt like a dampener had been put on what had been an amazing honeymoon. We were due to go home the next day anyway, so we saw no point in searching for a doctor abroad.

Back in England, a sonographer spread the gel across my stomach while I lay in silence on the table. She started to search for the baby on the screen, the quiet of the small room almost screaming at me. *It's hopeless*, I thought. *The baby's gone.* Emile watched the screen but I couldn't bear it, choosing to stare instead at the facing wall. Suddenly, a whooshing heartbeat filled the room. I snapped my head to the monitor: there in black and white was a tiny baby.

'There are big, black areas on the scan that I can see,' a doctor explained to us. 'That's a collection of blood forming.'

'What does that mean for the baby?' I asked, holding my breath nervously.

'Well, to be frank, we don't know,' the doctor admitted. 'Either the blood will get absorbed or it will come out. If it comes out, it may take the baby with it, but for now, the baby looks absolutely fine.'

'OK,' I said, accepting the news. 'There's still hope.'

The drive home from the hospital felt like a small victory, but what lay ahead of me was a painfully difficult pregnancy. Every few weeks I haemorrhaged, rushing to hospital with completely uncontrollable bleeding. *Am I losing the baby?* I panicked, but each time that small heartbeat would appear and the doctors would put the bleeding down to a threatened miscarriage. It was exhausting and emotionally draining. Initially, I'd just be in hospital for the day or for an overnight stay because I was still so early in the pregnancy that, if I did lose the baby, they wouldn't do anything to intervene. Reaching the twenty-eight-week mark felt like a huge weight off my shoulders, knowing that the doctors would try to save my baby if the worst were to happen. I was having regular scans to check that the baby was still growing.

Emile wanted to go away with some friends one weekend and, knowing that I was anxious at being left alone in case something went wrong, he bought me a teddy bear from Build-A-Bear. If you pressed the bear, its heart would beat for a few seconds. 'If you get scared,' Emile said, putting his arm round me, 'just listen to the bear's heartbeat and imagine it's our baby inside you.'

While this was happening, Emile was working towards selection for the Royal Army Physical Training Corps, which is a rigorous process. I supported him as best I could, using my experience in the army to help him with essay writing, current affairs discussions and how to conduct himself as a sergeant, which is what he would become if selected. To keep up with his sporting skills we would climb on an indoor wall in the evenings, and we'd often be joined by my work colleague and his friend, Chris, along with his girlfriend. A week or so after one such evening, Emile received a text from his line manager. He went white and just stared into the distance. I took the phone from him and read it. Chris had been climbing off the coast near Weymouth with his girlfriend when his gear had failed during a fall. He had plummeted to his death. I was surprised by how deeply this seemed to affect Emile, and for days he completely lost his confidence and wanted to withdraw from the selection course. Ultimately he attended and was successful, moving to Gibraltar Barracks in Minley to take up his new post, but I don't think he ever fully got over what had happened to Chris.

I had a regular scan booked for the day I finished work to go on maternity leave in April 2012. But we were faced with terrible news.

'The baby has stopped growing,' the consultant told Emile and me.

'What do we do?' Emile asked.

'There's a couple of options,' he replied. 'We can leave it a few days and see what happens—'

'No,' I interrupted. I was thirty-six weeks pregnant and I wasn't about to let anything happen to this baby now. 'If the baby isn't growing then there's something wrong, I want the baby born.'

'Looks like you're becoming parents today,' he nodded. They wheeled me into a different part of the hospital to be induced while Emile was sent off in a panic to buy the essentials for the baby.

'What do we need?' he asked as he headed for the door.

'Um, everything,' I replied, almost laughing. Given the constant threat of miscarriage and the previous loss of a pregnancy, I had refused to let myself and Emile become too prepared. I wanted to buy things for the baby but I couldn't bring myself to do it, and every time I had ventured to the shops, I'd avoided the baby section. I couldn't face the thought of the worst happening and having to return home to a house full of baby clothes and paraphernalia. Once he'd done his shopping trip, Emile found me in the hospital and stayed with me while I waited through the long process of being induced. The labour finally kicked in, but even then it seemed like it was never going to end. After hours of enduring the excruciating pain, it felt as though labour had stalled.

'I can't take any more of this,' I told the midwife as I lay in agony. 'I need the epidural.'

The midwife agreed and went to organize the epidural for me. But as soon as she left, suddenly I felt the baby's head beginning to crown. *Oh no. If I tell them they won't let me have the epidural*, I thought in my slightly delirious state. Yearning for any kind of pain relief, I kept quiet. A doctor administered the drug, but it was completely redundant by now as the baby was ready to be born.

'One final push, Vicky,' the midwife encouraged me, and I glanced over at Emile holding my hand by my side.

'You can do it,' he said.

Exhausted, I gave it all I had and after a few seconds, I heard the incredible sound of a baby's cry.

'Congratulations, you have a girl!'

Our perfect baby girl was born weighing 4lb 1oz and, listening to her screams, an incredible sense of relief washed over me. *People can help me look after her now.* After months of an isolating and terrifying pregnancy, it was comforting to know that someone else could take over. *I'm exhausted*, I realized. *I just want to be on my own.* Emile took hold of the baby, making sure she had skin-to-skin contact, while the doctors tried to remove my placenta.

'The placenta isn't coming out naturally,' they explained. 'So we're going to have to wheel you down to theatre.'

I nodded sleepily, peering over at Emile as I was taken out of the room. He leant back in his chair, our tiny baby resting peacefully on his chest. Emile's chin placed ever so gently on top of the baby's head, he looked up, smiling at me before I was wheeled out of sight. *I can relax now – Emile will look after us.*

# 4

# Growing a Family

'April is the perfect name for a perfect baby,' Emile cooed over our new arrival, making a big deal of her.

'It is,' I smiled, so full of love. We were settling into family life with ease, and I couldn't help but beam with pride over how great Emile was as a father. *He's so good with her*, I thought, watching him fuss over the newborn. Seeing him engage so well with our little girl, laughing and pulling faces, made me want to pretend that everything in our life was indeed perfect. We were in the hospital for two weeks whilst April had help with feeding and started to gain weight. Emile came in every day and spent as long as he could with us, helping me out with the feeding routine so I could get some rest. Our first family 'date' was dinner in the hospital restaurant, after I'd been given clearance to take April out of the maternity ward for a few hours. A simple act, but I couldn't imagine being happier.

Yet simmering away in the background were our ever-growing financial issues. At first, it seemed hardly worth mentioning. I noted the small amounts being withdrawn every now and again from our joint account, but everything else was going so well that it seemed unnecessary to bring it up. *It's just been an expensive few months.* I put it down to the costs of a newborn. *We'll start to build the savings back up again.*

I tried my best to shrug it off, hoping Emile would sort it all out. *He knows he's taken the money out so surely he's planning to put it back in*, I thought, assuming he would be able to deal with his finances. I decided not to bring it up and we coasted along, until one day I noticed a red bill amongst the morning post that I couldn't ignore. *That's odd.* I picked it up, tearing the envelope open. Inside was a warning letter from Next claiming that I hadn't paid for my latest order. *What?* I panicked. *But I haven't bought anything in months.* I rushed to log into my Next account. Scrolling through the list of items I apparently owed money for, I didn't recognize a single thing. *I've never seen these clothes before.*

'Emile,' I asked, wandering over to the kitchen, 'have you been buying stuff on my Next account?'

'What?' Emile quickly snapped, and his tone took me by surprise. 'Why would I do that?'

'It's nothing,' I replied, hovering by the door, shocked by his reaction. 'It's just that someone has been using my account.'

'And you think I would do that?' Emile said, his voice rising. I jolted. 'You seriously think I would use your account?' I couldn't believe how badly he was taking it.

'Well, no . . .' I paused, at a loss for what to say. 'I just wondered if you might have.'

'Someone must have hacked into your account,' Emile spat back, shaking his head. 'I can't believe you'd think I would do that.'

'Possibly,' I agreed, and suddenly I began to feel guilty for doubting him. The items that had been bought, jeans and a belt, had been purchased a while ago and I had never seen Emile wearing them. 'I'll tell Next I've been hacked.'

'I think you should.' Emile's tone was cutting as he stormed out of the kitchen. *I've offended him*, I realized, and I wished I had never mentioned it, especially when he continued to give me the cold shoulder until I couldn't take it any more and apologized.

I cancelled the account but, despite telling Next it wasn't me, I was still liable for the money owed. *I'd better not press his buttons further*, I thought, deciding against bringing it up again with Emile. I footed the outstanding bill and closed the account so that it couldn't happen again. I tried to ignore the niggling feeling I had over the way Emile had reacted, brushing it off as nothing more than a silly tiff, but little money incidents started to crop up more and more. Every few months my phone would be cut off for an unpaid bill, and I'd realize there was no money in our joint account. As more red letters came through the door, Emile always had an excuse ready for me. I even found paperwork that showed Emile had taken out an overdraft in my name and, eventually, a loan.

'There was a mix-up at work and I wasn't paid on time,' he insisted. 'They forgot to process my wages for this month.'

'So is that why you've taken out a loan on our joint account?' I tried to ask, but any hint I gave that I didn't completely believe him led to Emile flying off the handle.

'You don't trust me!' he shouted. 'You think I'm capable of lying like that and taking your money without consent?'

As much as I wanted to shout back, it just wasn't worth it. I had learnt by now that if I challenged him, Emile would sulk for days on end, barely speaking to me and making things very uncomfortable. I couldn't live like that, so I would always crack first and make an effort to bring him round again. Instead of tackling Emile, I let our financial problems fester.

I tried to rationalize it to myself. *What marriage doesn't have money worries? Although, it wasn't an issue I experienced with Liam.* Every so often I would send Emile the money to pay off any overdrafts he had opened, in an attempt to clear our debts. *We don't argue about anything else.*

'I've put a grand in your account,' I told him, hoping to get our finances back on track. 'So you can get rid of the loan.'

'OK, great,' he replied.

When I checked our accounts a few days later, I saw the overdraft was still outstanding. We were back to square one. No matter what I did, the money always seemed to disappear, and every time I tried to talk to Emile about it, he wouldn't listen.

I suspected Emile was spending money on his hobbies – he'd been into photography for a while, but now he was more into climbing and cricket again. I'd never see the bills though, and if I did spot what looked like a new piece of equipment, he'd tell me he'd bought it second-hand or a friend had lent it to him. He tended to keep things in his car or at work, so it was hard for me to keep track of what he was doing. If there was no physical evidence that he had bought an item, I couldn't face the stress and arguments of bringing it up. I was just confused. Confused about whether to believe my instinct or believe my husband.

*I want to trust the man I'm married to*, I thought to myself. Emile was loving with me and incredible with April, and so as the months passed I tried not to worry about the accounts.

'Do you think we should move house?' Emile suggested in the summer of 2013. The house I had bought a few years ago was old and not child-safe in the slightest. I noted how the property had been built on a slope and, with a couple of steep drops in the garden, I was constantly petrified of April getting hurt.

'Can we even afford to buy right now?' I replied, mulling over our current financial situation.

'I'll ring the bank to make an appointment,' Emile said, set on the fresh start. I imagined leaving our small, two-up two-down house and moving somewhere bigger where we could grow our family. At the meeting with the bank, though, it became apparent that Emile's money troubles were following us.

'I'm sorry but we can't offer you a mortgage,' the advisor told us. 'Not with this rating.' Amongst the loans and unpaid bills, all in my name, my credit rating had taken a nosedive. Listening as the advisor sifted through our catalogue of poor finances, my cheeks flushed red. *How embarrassing*, I thought to myself, almost wincing at the amount of money we owed. I had always been so careful with my savings, but Emile was draining them.

'What are we going to do?' I asked Emile on the way home.

'We could use your inheritance,' he suggested. My gran had died recently, and both my brother Christopher and I had inherited some money.

'I don't even think that money would cover the costs of a new house,' I admitted. 'I just don't think moving is feasible right now.' As much as I wanted a nicer home for April, listening to the advisor at the bank had shocked me into a reality check.

'Well, why don't you see if Christopher will help you out?' Emile continued, and I knew he wasn't going to let this go.

'I can't just ask my brother for that kind of money,' I retorted.

'Not to keep, no,' Emile reasoned. 'But to borrow.'

*That might be a good idea*, I thought, and Christopher

happily agreed to help us buy a new home. Instead of paying off a mortgage, we would pay my brother back each month, although he and my dad insisted that the deed to the house be in my name only and that Emile and I would sign a post-nuptial agreement. If we were to divorce then we would leave the marriage with what we had put in. With so much of mine and my family's money tied up in the house, they wanted to be sure I would keep it if my marriage broke down.

We quickly found the perfect house, a newbuild with an enclosed garden where April could safely play, and was near a park. As much as I liked it, I did worry that the amount we would owe Christopher each month was a lot more than we would be able to comfortably pay.

'What if we applied for planning permission for this house instead?' I suggested to Emile. 'I know it wouldn't be great to live in while the building work is going on around us, but it's doable.' I paused for a second. 'And it will be much cheaper.'

'No.' Emile shook his head, adamant about the move. 'The other house will be better for bringing up kids.'

'I'm just thinking of saving us money,' I told him. *Can we afford any more debt?*

'I'll pay the majority of the money back to your brother each month,' Emile offered. 'That way you're not worrying.'

'Are you sure?' I asked, surprised by the suggestion.

'Of course,' he replied. I thought back to the debts and unpaid bills. *Emile will never pay all of that money back to my brother*, I thought to myself. Christopher had already been so generous to lend us the amount in the first place, and I worried Emile's unreliability could cause a rift in the family.

'Transfer it into my account each month and I'll pay it to Christopher,' I decided. *That way if he doesn't come through on his promise, Christopher doesn't have to know.* And for the first few months after the move, our payment plan worked well. But then I started to get missed transfers.

'There was a mix-up with my wages,' Emile told me, shrugging when I questioned him about the money.

'Again?' I asked in disbelief.

'Yeah,' he simply replied, nodding. *You must be lying*, I thought, staring him in the eye, but he didn't flinch. *But how am I supposed to prove it?*

'You should probably complain,' I told him, unconvinced. 'That's not acceptable.' Emile just shrugged.

'It'll get sorted,' he replied. Once again, I had no option but to take Emile's word for it, and bit by bit all of the monthly bills fell to me. *At least this way he can't take any more loans out*, I told myself.

Another issue that was surfacing was my involvement with the parachute centre. I was reliant on the money I earnt as an instructor there to help pay for the mortgage, especially when Emile's contribution fell short, so I was at the airfield most weekends. When I had fallen pregnant with April the jumping had stopped, but I still taught ground school and tried to keep my skills up as much as I could. But after giving birth, the sport had changed for me. It had gone from being a fun hobby to something that was more of a job and, with a growing family, my priorities had changed.

*I just don't enjoy jumping any more*, I realized. *I've lost the spark for it.* I didn't know if the problems going on at home were reflected in my feelings towards the sport, but I partly blamed skydiving for my issues with Emile. *It takes me away from home too often*, I told myself. *I need to focus on April and Emile.* Now a mother, I was more aware of the dangers surrounding the jumps, worried something would happen to me and I wouldn't be able to take care of my daughter. Cracks were starting to show in my marriage to Emile and so I decided to cut down my hours at the parachute centre, and focus on our relationship.

The biggest draw for me to move to the bigger house was that we could expand our family. By now, I was thirty-eight years old and already reaching the limit of my fertility. *How will we cope financially with another baby?* Emile was spending our money faster than I could save anything, but I imagined our life with two kids. *We'd be a perfect family.*

When I broached the subject to Emile, he was over the moon.

'Let's have another baby,' he beamed, and I swept the money troubles to one side. *I'll just have to make my salary stretch.* Overjoyed, Emile threw his arms around me, and just like that I fell back into our idyllic bubble.

'Perhaps we'll have another girl to be friends with April,' I imagined, daydreaming of the two girls running hand in hand.

'Or a little boy so that we have one of each,' Emile added. I couldn't wait to complete our family, but after nearly a year of trying I still hadn't fallen pregnant and, concerned, I booked an appointment to speak to a doctor.

'We're just going to do some baseline tests,' the consultant told me at my GP surgery. Emile was working and so couldn't come with me. 'The tests will check your hormone levels and we'll take some blood as well.'

'OK,' I answered. 'And what happens then?'

'Well, we'll need a sperm sample from your husband.' The doctor handed me a sample pot. 'Take this, and here's some leaflets for more information. Get your husband to come back in with the sample and we can take it from there.'

'Emile is with a different medical centre,' I replied, taking the paperwork from him.

'That's fine, just have them send over the results.'

'OK, thank you.'

I left the doctor's feeling positive that after months of trying we were finally progressing, and when Emile returned home from work, I handed over the sample pot and leaflets. I tried to keep my hopes high and, after a couple of weeks, I was called back in to attend a review appointment.

'You'll need to bring the results from your husband's

test along with you as well,' the receptionist told me over the phone.

'Of course,' I replied, hanging up the phone. 'Emile,' I said, walking through to where he was sitting in the living room, playing with April. 'Did you go to the doctors with the sample?'

'Yes,' he answered, preoccupied.

'What did they say?' I asked, trying to get to the bottom of it.

'It's been checked and it's fine.' He glanced up at me for a second.

'Well, I need a print-off or something to take back to the doctors with me.'

'I don't have anything to give you.' Emile bounced April on his knee.

'They didn't give you any paperwork?' I asked, and he shook his head. I suspected he hadn't been tested but I couldn't face having an argument with him, which would be the inevitable result of me pressing the issue, so I was left to go to the doctors without Emile's results.

*Why doesn't he care?* I suddenly felt like crying as I drove alone to the appointment. *He knows how important this is to me.* The doctors referred me to a fertility specialist, but about a week before I was due to see the consultant, I had an inkling. With no rational reason, just a suspicion, I went to the shops to buy a pregnancy test. I went home and ran to the bathroom, all the while trying not to get my hopes up.

Seeing the positive sign light up, I nearly screamed

with excitement. I burst out of the bathroom and hurried to the kitchen, where Emile was eating lunch with April.

'That's great news,' he smiled, but while he did seem happy, he lacked the ecstatic excitement he had shown when I had fallen pregnant with April. As quickly as it had appeared, Emile's smile vanished from his face and he turned back to his lunch. I stood still, pregnancy test in hand, wishing he would stand up to give me a hug. It felt like a definitive shift and, shortly afterwards, things noticeably changed.

A friend's sixteen-year-old daughter had done some babysitting for us on the odd occasion and, when she rang me out of the blue one afternoon, I assumed we must have forgotten to pay her.

'This is really awkward,' I listened to my friend sigh down the phone. 'But I think your husband's been asking inappropriate questions and sending lots of messages to my daughter.'

'What?' The accusation knocked me for six. 'Emile wouldn't do that.' But as the screenshots were sent to my phone, one by one, I was stunned into silence.

*Do you have a boyfriend?* A text from Emile read. *You look really nice this evening*. I felt as if the world was going to drop from under me, my stomach plummeting and my hands shaking. It was familiar to me, the same shocked disbelief I'd felt when Liam cheated and my life turned upside down.

'I'm so sorry,' I muttered down the phone. 'I'll speak to Emile.' I couldn't imagine there would be a way for him to talk himself out of it, but when I confronted Emile about the text messages he insisted it wasn't true.

'My phone must have been cloned.' Emile's voice rose as he spoke. 'It's got nothing to do with me.'

'How would your phone be cloned?' I snapped back.

'Well, my Apple account must have been hacked or something,' he replied, adamant that he hadn't sent the texts. 'How could you think that of me?'

'The messages are right there.' I showed him the screenshots.

'How can you not believe me?' Emile shouted back, his tone growing aggressive. 'Do you really think that little of me?'

'I want to believe you,' I started to back-track. *Why would Emile want to flirt with our teenage babysitter?* It felt entirely out of character. 'It must have been a mistake.'

'I'm going out.' Emile stormed out of the house. For a few minutes, I didn't move, rereading the messages on my phone. *He can't have done this*, I thought, feeling guilty for ever accusing him. *I should have trusted him.*

The next morning I left the house with April to go to the childminder and then on to work, only to discover that Emile had taken my car.

'Typical,' I muttered, forced to use Emile's older car, which was parked out the front. Sliding into the driver's seat, I looked over at the glove compartment and, without thinking, reached over to open it. The empty sample pot and paperwork from the doctor's surgery fell out onto the passenger seat. *He never did see the GP about his fertility*, I realized, letting my head fall into my hands. *He lied to me*. But I never broached that topic with him. I was pregnant now and it simply wasn't worth muddying the water.

A few days later, some messages from Emile's email account popped up on the family computer. I glanced at the subject heading, not intending to click on the message, but as soon as I'd seen who it was from, I couldn't look away. *He's receiving emails from a sex club*.

'Oh.' Emile paused when I confronted him about it, and he seemed to be taken aback for a split-second before the stoic look on his face reappeared. 'Well, they just send me messages every so often because I used to go there with my ex-wife.'

'Oh, right,' I answered, disgusted by his response as he was clearly lying. Why would they suddenly start messaging many years later when he had new email accounts and a new phone number? 'Nice.' I tried to dismiss it as nothing, but a week later more messages appeared on the computer. *I had a great time tonight*, the message from an unknown woman read. *Yeah, me too*, Emile had replied. *It's just as well there was that security camera in the car park, otherwise who knows what would have happened*. I was gobsmacked and, furious, I confronted Emile.

'I knew you were lying,' I snapped, showing him the texts.

'My account has been hacked,' he quickly replied.

'I'm not stupid, Emile.' I felt tears prick at the corners of my eyes. 'Your account hasn't been hacked.'

'Don't put your own issues onto me.' Emile's tone was condescending. 'Just because your ex-husband cheated on you doesn't mean you can be paranoid with me.'

*Why is he being like this with me?* I wondered, but slowly I started to worry that he was right. *What if I am paranoid?* He would often spend hours making dinners that he thought we would both enjoy, getting a bottle of wine and a movie to watch afterwards. He rarely went out or showed much interest in going out. I just couldn't imagine him going to a sex club. Then I found a receipt in Emile's jeans from Nando's. It was for two meals, and one order – a glass of white wine and a salad – looked distinctly female.

'It's not mine,' Emile insisted, adamant the paper had mistakenly ended up in his pocket.

I was determined to catch him out in his lie. My chance came one day when April was sick on the carpet after dinner.

'It's no good,' Emile said, giving up after scrubbing at the carpet. 'I'll go buy some proper carpet cleaner.' When he came home, I fished the receipt out of the bag to find the same card had been used both at the shop and at Nando's.

'Wow, Vicky.' Emile flew off the handle as soon as I mentioned it. 'I think you're losing it.'

'I'm not,' I tried to protest, but he wouldn't let me speak.

'This is all because of your insecurities with your ex-husband, and now you're checking my receipts.' When he put it like that, it did sound ludicrous. I looked down at the receipts in my hands and began to doubt myself.

'I'm sorry,' I replied, trying to calm him down. 'But you said you hadn't gone to Nando's.'

'I'm not talking about this,' Emile dismissed me. 'You're crazy.' It was as though my loving, doting husband had been replaced by someone else.

My bump was growing by the week, but every scan and appointment I needed to attend at the hospital, I went to alone.

'You know how busy I am.' Emile let out an exaggerated sigh. 'I can't just drop work because you have a scan.'

'I know,' I mumbled, too tired and pregnant to argue back. I was still working full-time as well as juggling childcare for April and preparing for our arrival, and without Emile's help I was exhausted. But the worst thing was my constant fear that at any moment I might start haemorrhaging, as I had done with April. I had monthly scans and my pregnancy was totally normal, but I could not relax.

As my bump continued to grow, so did our money problems. Small amounts were still periodically being removed from my savings accounts – the sums were increasing, as was the frequency with which the money disappeared. I was concerned, but whenever I voiced it

Emile had an excuse ready, and it was always somewhat viable. Whether it was a mix-up at the bank or a mistake with his wages, I knew there was no way for me to prove Emile was lying. *Hopefully it won't happen again*, I thought, noticing £500 had suddenly vanished from my account. *Emile will sort it out*, I told myself. But he didn't, and more issues just kept cropping up. It caused me many sleepless nights worrying about how I would make ends meet each month. I was paying for the loan, the childcare, the food and all of the bills by this stage, despite the fact that he earnt more than me.

'I think your card has been cloned or stolen,' he suggested to me when I tried to raise the problem one day.

'I should tell the bank and get the card cancelled then,' I replied, waiting to see if Emile would react, but he simply shrugged.

'That's probably for the best.' I phoned up the bank, telling them payments had been made without my authorization, and they sent out a replacement card. I waited a few days for the new one to arrive, but by the end of two weeks I was still without a credit card.

'That's weird,' I commented to Emile, checking my online banking. 'Money is still going out.'

'Maybe the post was intercepted,' he replied. 'And someone took your card.'

'Maybe,' I answered, not believing a word he said. *Or maybe you've taken it*, I thought.

One afternoon, I was searching through Emile's paperwork and found my missing credit card stashed away in his Filofax. *I knew it*, I thought, angry at yet another lie. I understood there was no point in confronting Emile about it, as there would always be someone else for him to blame. Instead, I decided I needed to be more careful, changing my passwords and closing my online banking. I made it so that the only way for me to withdraw money was to physically go into the bank with my passport, but Emile still found a way to siphon off our savings. His mother was ill in hospital at one point and needed to settle her bill before she could leave, plus her medication was expensive. Emile came to me looking sheepish, and said he was going to sell some stuff so he could give his dad £1,000 to help out. That seemed wrong to me – we were married, our money was shared, and I wasn't going to refuse to help his parents.

'Don't be ridiculous, I'll send your dad the money. You don't need to sell anything,' I said.

'He'd be too proud to take money from you, Vicky,' Emile replied. 'It's best if he thinks it comes from me.'

Knowing his dad, I thought that made sense. It was only later that I found out only half of the money actually made it to South Africa.

I was desperately trying to protect myself and my child from Emile's impulsive and irresponsible behaviour, but even that didn't feel right. *I shouldn't have to live like this*, I seethed. *I should be able to trust my husband.*

I knew that our marriage couldn't continue like this, but I was scared at that point to face bringing up and fully supporting a baby and a toddler. I knew that if I ended the relationship any support – physical and financial – that I was getting, at times, would end.

On top of our money troubles, Emile was finding more and more reasons not to be at home. He cleared off whenever he could, volunteering for duties over the weekend or signing up to compete with the skydiving team. He was on a trip with the British Skydiving Nationals when I saw pictures on Facebook of him cosying up to various women. Sitting at home with April and my pregnancy bump, I felt foolish. *These people know me*, I groaned, mortified. *They must think I'm a moron.* The photos weren't overtly terrible, but seeing him clearly drunk with his arms draped around another woman felt inappropriate. I had heard nothing from him while he had been away, but I could see he was having a good enough time without me. When my phone rang the next morning, it was the first time Emile had tried to contact me for days.

'Hi,' I answered, surprised to be hearing from him.

'Hi Vicky, I need you to pick me up,' he quickly replied. 'My car has been impounded.'

'What?' I asked in disbelief. 'Why?'

'It wasn't insured – it's just a mistake,' he said. 'Can you come and get me?' After I finished work that evening, I drove north to pick him up from his skydiving trip. The car had been impounded because Emile hadn't paid the insurance on it, but he swore blind it wasn't his fault.

'The insurers have messed up,' he told me when I got there. 'But my car can't be released until I pay for it.' Ultimately, I knew I would be the one to pay for his car and when I did, I didn't get so much as a thank you. We returned home and it felt like the wheels of our relationship were about to fall off.

A night we spent at a friend's party only confirmed it further. It was the middle of the evening when, with everyone's phones lying around unnoticed, one of the screens flashed up. A friend picked up the phone with a smirk on her face.

'Someone's got a Tinder match,' she laughed before raising her voice. 'Whose phone is this?' Only hearing the last half of the sentence, Emile looked over at her.

'That's my phone,' he replied, turning back to his conversation.

'Oh,' she muttered, glancing at me as she rested the phone back down. I felt my cheeks turn red, embarrassed. It was just one of the many moments in our relationship when I felt completely sick. *Not again*, I wanted to cry. Once home, I downloaded the dating app in a bid to find him, but when he noticed what I was doing, he immediately lost his temper.

'You don't trust me,' he accused. 'You're trying to catch me out.' *That's quite a guilty response*, I thought to myself.

'Why do you have Tinder then?' I asked, and I waited for the inevitable excuse.

'My mates stuck me on it for a laugh,' he replied,

sighing in exasperation at me. 'You just have issues,' he added, yet again blaming my suspicions on the infidelity in my first marriage. His comment stung. *Does he really have such little respect for me?* I wondered. *That he feels he can treat me like this.* He wasn't even trying to be subtle now, and it felt like the more trapped I became, especially with the pregnancy, the worse he behaved with me.

'I'm going away for a few weeks,' Emile announced in October. 'It's a ski trip with work.'

I knew that a lot of training, including skiing, went on in November and December, but I felt put out by the news.

'Oh. I like skiing too, you know.' Being pregnant meant that I wouldn't be able to take part in the sport, but Emile's trip only made the rift between us more apparent.

'Well, you can come out for a few days,' Emile shrugged, but I shook my head.

'I need to stay here to look after April,' I told him, turning down what I knew to be an empty gesture. *He wouldn't want me there anyway.*

'OK,' Emile replied. 'I leave for Austria in a couple of days.'

'Oh,' I mumbled, at a loss for what to say.

*Don't go*, I screamed internally. *Stay here and help me.* And while I knew that all I had to do was tell him, I wanted Emile to choose his family over a ski trip by himself, not because he had to. But it was no use – after a few days, Emile left me with everything else to deal with by myself. Facing the next few weeks alone, I was petrified that I would bleed and miscarry again, and emotionally I couldn't cope, constantly bursting into tears over the slightest thing. *I wish Emile would just come back*, I thought, but I wanted the person I had fallen in love with, not the man Emile had now become. Even over text, Emile was distant. Occasionally, he would phone to speak to April, but he never wanted to talk to me. The only time he ever really contacted me was when he wanted to sext. Emile had no interest in how I was coping.

*I just need someone to hug me*, I thought as I cried in front of the TV one evening. *I just wish someone would tell me that they love me.* Juggling my job and taking care of April, with her terrible twos in full swing, was almost too much to bear, and during one of my visits to the hospital I suddenly broke down, sobbing uncontrollably. The midwife doing my check-up looked concerned.

'Is something wrong at home?' she asked, comforting me until I calmed down. *I think my husband is being unfaithful*, I wanted to say.

'My husband's away at the moment and it's all a bit much,' I choked. *I don't think he loves me any more*, I added internally. *He just uses me for money.*

'It's going to be OK.' She gave my hand a squeeze but the worried look on her face didn't go away. 'I'm going to email your regular midwife so she can help you.'

'Thanks,' I replied, wishing I could tell her what was really going on.

On one of Emile's calls, he bluntly asked, 'What do you want for Christmas? I may as well get my presents while I'm in Austria.'

'Um . . .' I tried to think of something easy for him to pick up. 'Some slippers perhaps, or a box of chocolates.'

'I don't have much money,' he replied. *Slippers aren't expensive*, I thought.

'Well, if it's that bad, I can give you some money,' I offered, but he refused.

'No, it's fine, I'll talk to you later.' And with that, Emile put the phone down. I shrugged the conversation off. *At least he's thinking of me.* I decided to take the chat as a positive sign.

At the same time, the fact Emile was so hopeless with money had brought me to a decision. Childbirth is not without risk, and I wanted the peace of mind that if something happened to me, the children would have some financial support when they came of age. So in December I changed my will, dividing my estate between the children. I knew that Emile would get housing and support from the army and he had a decent job.

Emile didn't come home until two days before Christmas, so I was left to do all of the preparations myself. When he did finally return, he was a different person. Where Emile had been uninterested before, he was now completely dismissive of me. He spent any family time together glued to his phone, ignoring any attempt I made at conversation and lying unnecessarily about everything.

'When did you start smoking?' I asked, noticing the distinct smell of cigarettes on his clothes.

'I'm not smoking,' Emile insisted. *You're lying*, I thought.

'Oh, my mistake,' I replied, but I had already seen the ash scattered around his car and, a few days later, the packet of cigs he had hidden in his coat pocket. *What's the use in challenging him?* I thought to myself. *He'll only deny it.*

We both had a couple of weeks off work together during the Christmas break. I decided to make the most of it, determined not to argue with him. Driving down to my stepsister's in London for Christmas Day, I felt quietly positive. *Now is the perfect time for us to reconnect*, I thought. *No distractions.* But even with our family, Emile just wasn't present, burying his head in his phone and ignoring whatever was going on around him. My parents, stepsister and her husband were all chatting in the living room while Emile sat in the corner, typing away on his phone.

'Let's go out for a walk,' I suggested to him, but he shook his head, not even peering up to look at me. *Who are you talking to?* I wondered, a part of me wanting to just grab the phone from his hands and throw it out of the window. Curious about what was captivating Emile's attention, I took any rare chance I could to glance at his locked phone screen, and each time I did, I saw the name Stefanie pop up. *He doesn't know anyone called Stefanie*, I thought, realizing that I didn't know anything about my husband's life any more.

When Christmas morning came, I lifted April out of her cot to sit with Emile in bed. He took her from me, playing with her while I fetched the presents. I had filled a stocking for him and had helped April to make him a card, but as I presented them Emile's face fell. Opening the gifts in his stocking, he went quiet.

'What's the matter?' I asked him.

'I haven't got anything for you,' Emile told me, and my heart sank. 'Well, I ordered you something but it never came.'

'Oh,' I replied. *He doesn't care enough to get me a Christmas present.*

'And I didn't have much money,' Emile added, but that only made me feel worse. *I don't want you to spend lots of money*, I thought. *A card made by April would have meant more to me than anything else.* I didn't say anything, knowing deep down that the real reason Emile hadn't bought me anything was because he didn't care to.

'It doesn't matter,' I lied, but my disappointment turned into embarrassment as the morning wore on and I sat empty-handed, watching everyone else open their gifts. *I mean so little to Emile that I didn't even warrant a £5 box of chocolates.* My stepsister's husband had bought her lots of little thoughtful presents, all individually wrapped, and he sat excitedly as he watched her open them. I felt like there was a neon sign pointing at me saying, *My husband didn't so much as get me a card.* Mortified, I helped April open her presents, trying to distract myself from the fact that I was the only one in the room with nothing to open. With all the excited commotion from the children, no one seemed to notice. *This is one of the worst days of my life*, I thought, willing the ground to swallow me up.

But just when I didn't think things could get any worse, Emile stunned me with an announcement.

'I'm going away again for a couple of weeks,' he told me nonchalantly. 'I'll be gone over New Year.'

'What?' I asked, shocked by this sudden revelation. 'I thought we were going to spend New Year together and have some time off.'

'But it's work,' Emile's excuses rang out. 'I've got to run a course over in Germany.'

'No one works over New Year,' I replied, not buying his sudden work trip. 'You know, I've not really seen you since October.'

'Well, it's the reserves,' he replied, but having spent years in the military, I knew not even the reserves worked over the holiday season. 'It's last minute, but doing these kinds of things will help me towards getting support for my British passport.' Suddenly it felt like he was guilt-tripping me into agreeing with him.

'Well, I suppose that is important,' I replied. Inside, I knew Emile was up to something but I was also seven months pregnant. *What can I do?* Deflated, I didn't argue any further and, watching him pack, it seemed like he couldn't wait to go away again.

'Don't be gone too long,' I smiled, holding on to my baby bump. 'We still need to pick out a name for this one.'

'I'll be back when I can,' Emile replied, scooping April up for a cuddle. I waved him out of the door with a sick feeling in my stomach.

'Just me and you again,' I cooed to April, ruffling her hair. Emile hadn't long left when the phone rang and I wandered over to pick it up.

'This is a notification from Lloyds Bank. There are transactions on your credit card that have bounced back due to insufficient funding.' I felt my face burning as I listened to the flight details and currency exchange Emile had tried to buy with my card. Afterwards, I gave him a call.

'I told you it was a last-minute work thing.' Emile sounded angry on the phone. 'I have to pay for the tickets and work will pay me back.' He didn't ask me for money so he must have found it somewhere. After he hung up, I slumped down onto the floor with April. *I'm trapped*, I realized. *My husband doesn't love me and I'm trapped.*

# 5

# The Gas Leak

Once Emile had left for his trip, I didn't hear anything from him for the first couple of days. *God, I hope he's all right*, I worried to myself. *What if something happens to him?* Heavily pregnant and left alone to take care of our two-year-old, I sought advice from a friend who had once been posted at the same base as Emile in Germany.

'I'm just a bit concerned about him,' I admitted to her over the phone. 'And I know you used to be posted at Paderborn.'

'Oh, he's at Paderborn?' she answered calmly. 'He should be fine, it's a massive site and the whole camp is wired up to the internet.'

'Ah, I see,' I responded, embarrassed that I'd even mentioned it. 'That's good.' *I never should have phoned her*, I berated myself. *Now she'll know something isn't right.*

'Is everything OK, Vicky?' she asked, but I was quick to gloss over it.

'Yes, of course, everything's fine,' I replied, trying my best to keep my voice as cool and collected as possible.

I couldn't bear the thought of anyone knowing the reality of our life at home. Once I was off the phone, I let out a sigh, cupping my face in my hands. *So it's just me he's ignoring then*, I thought to myself, disheartened to know the truth. Emile had full access to a phone signal but hadn't bothered to send me so much as a text. I tried to get on with the day-to-day of life, busying myself with work and April. After a few more days of radio silence, I eventually heard from Emile.

*The reception is really bad here in Paderborn*, he lamely tried to explain over a text. *There's no Wi-Fi.* Reading the message, my stomach tied into knots. *He's lying*, I realized, before typing back to him, *I see. I had thought Paderborn was good for signal.* I didn't have to wait long for a reply. *No, it's not, you probably won't hear much from me*, his cold text read. I couldn't believe how brazen Emile was being. Shaking my head, I put my phone back down, no longer wanting to talk to him. I couldn't understand why he had felt the need to lie. *What is he hiding from me?* I wondered. With no sign of Emile returning any time soon, I resigned myself to spending New Year's at home, but upon hearing this a friend from parachuting, Antoinette, wouldn't allow it.

'You're not spending New Year alone,' she insisted.

'It's fine,' I replied. 'I'll just stay home with April.'

'No, you won't,' Antoinette pushed, not taking no for an answer. 'At the very least, you can come to mine for dinner.'

'OK, fine,' I agreed, and I was touched that she cared.

On New Year's Eve, I headed round to my friend's house for her dinner party, taking April along with me.

'It won't be a late one for me,' I forewarned her, noticing my daughter tiredly rub her eyes. 'April isn't going to make it to midnight.'

'Bless her,' Antoinette cooed to a sleepy April, and we placed her to snooze on the sofa. When it was time to leave, I said my goodbyes with April offering hugs at the front door, before I strapped her safely into her car seat.

'Happy New Year, you two!' Antoinette beamed, waving at us as I pulled my car away from the drive. I drove us home in silence, glancing briefly in the mirror at my sleeping baby. *She's adorable*, I smiled to myself, wishing Emile was here to snap a picture of her. With the baby bump and two-year-old in tow, I had known New Year's Eve would be a quiet night, but I had never imagined I wouldn't have Emile for company. In those few minutes of calm, I suddenly felt a pang of loneliness. *He should be here with me*, I thought, saddened by the fact that such an important member of the family was absent. *He shouldn't want to miss this*. It would be our last New Year as a trio, a milestone that didn't seem to be significant to Emile. I let a couple of tears fall as I drove before pulling myself together. *I just have to get on with it*, I told myself. *What choice do I have?* Parking in our driveway, I gently lifted April from her seat and carried her up to bed.

'When you wake up it'll be a brand-new year,' I smiled, tucking April into bed. I planted a kiss on the top of her head and, seeing she was settled, I sneaked out of the room. Once alone, I plonked myself downstairs with a cup of tea and waited for the New Year's countdown. *I wonder what Emile is doing right now?* He had told me he was spending the night in Berlin but I had no idea who he was with. *He's so cagey about who he spends his time with*, I noted. Flicking through the TV channels, I settled on watching the celebrations happening in London. The ten-second countdown began.

'Ten, nine, eight,' the crowd chanted, and I imagined Emile partying away, pretending to be a single man. I watched the handle on the clock creep its way to midnight. 'Three, two, one!' The television blared with Big Ben's chimes and I glanced over at my phone. *He'll probably text me soon*, I thought. *After all, he is still my husband.* Exhausted from the day, I wanted to go to bed, but instead I stayed up, longing to hear from Emile. Checking my phone periodically, I hoped he would get in touch but each time I looked, a blank screen stared back at me. *Am I really not going to hear from him?* I began to wonder, my heart sinking as the night wore on. Watching the crowds of people celebrating on the telly, ringing in the New Year with their loved ones, I had never felt lonelier. Eventually, at 2 a.m., I gave up. Teary-eyed, I took myself off to bed. *He'll probably message me in the night*, I told myself. *I'll wake up to a message.* I knew it wouldn't really happen but as I fell asleep, I let myself believe Emile would care enough to get in touch. When I awoke the next morning, the first thing I did was grab my phone, but I still hadn't received any messages and my heart sank again. It wasn't until the afternoon of New Year's Day that my phone finally buzzed.

*Happy New Year*, the bland three-word message from Emile read. *Is that it?* I scoffed, upset by the lack of affection. *He really doesn't care, does he?* I shook my head and, ignoring the text message, I put my phone away. An hour later, it pinged again. *Oh, be like that then*, Emile wrote. Reading his sharp message, I paused, suddenly angry. *I know he's up to something over there, I'm not stupid. But I don't know what the hell is going on.* I thought back to the suspicious messages I had seen on Emile's phone, that he had been talking to a woman named Stefanie just before he left. *I know he's up to no good*, I thought. *But I can't tell anyone.*

It wasn't easy to get a chance for a real heart-to-heart with my friends. When Emile was around, he was quite watchful. He'd logged onto my iPad once and seen that I'd been sarcastic about him in a message to a friend. He blamed his snooping on April, saying she'd been playing on my iPad and he'd just happened to see the message. It led to some angry accusations from him, followed by the usual silent treatment. If friends called round to the house to see me, Emile would sit with us even if he wasn't taking part in the conversation. 'Can't you get rid of your husband?' one friend said jokingly. 'How can we have a good gossip with a man in the room.' Quite apart from that, I also knew that if I confided in any of my friends I'd have to deal with their shock at Emile's behaviour. I worried that they'd tell me I should leave him, and I just wasn't strong enough or ready to make that leap. Realizing I would have no choice but to keep this to myself, I felt my eyes start to prick. I spent New Year's Day in floods of tears, unable to deny the truth to myself any longer. *I think my husband is cheating on me.* The reality was devastating.

Putting April to bed that night, my eyes were red from crying.

'Are you sad?' she asked, squirming in her bed as I tried to settle her.

'No, darling,' I comforted her, forcing myself to smile as I kissed her goodnight.

'When is Daddy coming home?' April queried, and the knot in my stomach tightened.

'Soon,' I promised, stroking her hair. 'But first, you have to go to sleep.'

Struggling to my feet with my baby bump, I walked across the room and turned the light off. Slowly pulling April's door shut behind me, I stood in silence at the top of the stairs and burst into tears. Hunched over the banister, I cried, imagining Emile having the time of his life in Germany with another woman. As I sobbed, I felt the baby kick violently. *If I keep crying,* I suddenly realized, *I'm going to miscarry.* Standing still on the quiet landing, I felt myself slip into a dark place. *He probably wouldn't even care if I did lose the baby.* I thought back to how cold Emile had been before he left. *Would he even come back if I miscarried?* Suddenly, I felt a tiny pair of hands wrap around my legs.

'It's OK, Mummy,' April reassured me, squeezing my leg tightly. 'I'll look after you.'

'Thanks, sweetheart,' I choked, burying my face in my hands. I couldn't stop myself from crying.

'I'll look after you and the baby,' my little girl promised. I crumpled to the floor, wrapping April up in a hug. 'Daddy will come home soon,' she told me, and my heart dropped. *I can't believe I've got to this place*, I thought, knowing that I couldn't even hide the issues from April any more. *How has it come to this?* I willed myself to calm down before taking my daughter back to bed.

'Don't worry,' I cooed as I tucked her in. 'We're going to be fine, Mummy is fine.' I walked back out onto the landing. It felt like I was spending my life holding my breath, waiting for Emile to either snap back into family life or leave me for good. With nothing else to lose, I pulled out my phone and started typing. *I have loved you more each year*, I confessed to Emile, aching to spark any form of emotion from him. *It feels like you keep trying to push me away until I jump ship.* I pressed send and paused for a moment before adding, *But I can't. I love you too much. It just feels now that you would be happier without me.* I threw my phone down by my side, knowing by now not to expect a reply.

By the time Emile returned, I had barely talked to anyone but my two-year-old for two weeks, and they had been the loneliest weeks of my life. But even now, with Emile home, I may as well have been on my own. He avoided me altogether, choosing to spend time in whichever room I wasn't in. He was still interacting with April but it seemed as though he wanted nothing to do with me. One evening, we sat silently in the living room watching TV when my phone pinged. Picking it up from the arm of the sofa, I did a double-take. *Why has Emile sent me an email?* I glanced over at him on the other side of the couch, but he just stared blankly straight ahead at the TV. Baffled, I opened the message.

*Talking to you over email is a lot easier because you get too emotional when I talk to you face to face*, Emile had written. Instantly, I felt sick. *I'm not sure how I feel about the marriage.*

*I'm heavily pregnant!* I wanted to shout. *You've left me on my own, I know you're taking money from me, I know you're having an affair, and you think I'm being a bit emotional?* I took a deep breath and wrote out my reply. *You really do pick your timings*, I typed, biting my tongue.

*I'm not sure if I want to be married to you any more, I need some time out to think*, Emile replied. *I'll still be there for you and the baby though.*

'This is ridiculous.' I broke the silence, turning to face him. 'We can't just keep sending emails to each other, we need to talk about this.'

'OK.' Emile turned to me. 'But what is there to say?' I hesitated for a moment, knowing deep down the question I really wanted answering.

'Is there someone else?' I asked, and Emile looked me straight in the eye.

'No,' he stated firmly. *Then who is Stefanie?* I wondered but, too tired to listen to any excuses he had lined up, I kept quiet.

'I've been given a room at the base,' Emile started to tell me, and my heart plummeted. 'So I'm going to stay there while I'm working.' I nodded, all the while wanting to scream at him. *I'm about to give birth and I'm taking care of a toddler*, I imagined I'd say. *And you're leaving me again.*

'Can we just focus on having the baby right now?' I pleaded.

'Yes,' Emile agreed. 'We'll focus on the baby, but I think we'll need to talk. I'll stick by you for the first few months but then we should have a rethink about our relationship.' His words cut like a knife.

'Right,' I replied, at a loss for what to say.

Voicing my concerns didn't change anything and, evidently not wanting to be with me, Emile went away, reappearing every now and then on the weekends. It was as though he didn't want to be at home but he didn't quite want to let go and, for me, it felt cruel.

One night, struggling to walk, I slowly heaved myself up the stairs. It was a rare evening that Emile was home and, as I made my way into our bedroom, he decided to drop a further bombshell on me.

'I'm going on another trip,' Emile stated bluntly from his side of the bed. He paused, as if waiting for a response, but I didn't speak. 'It's just a military diving trip in May.'

'We'll have a newborn by then,' I commented, fighting back the sudden urge to cry. The days were ticking down to my due date.

'Well, no,' Emile objected, ignoring the hurt in my voice. 'The baby will be a few weeks old by then.' *He's going to leave me alone with two babies*, I panicked. The added stress meant the baby's activity had become unpredictable – some days it was hyperactive, kicking like crazy in my stomach, and other days I didn't feel a thing, which I knew was a bad sign.

Emile shrugged and he didn't mention it again, but on the family computer I found emails he had sent to his instructor. *What is the arrangement for accommodation?* he had asked about the diving trip. *I'm planning to bring my girlfriend.* Each word on the screen was like a dagger. On the shared internet history I discovered searches for sex and fetish clubs in the local area, and further afield whenever he'd been away. I felt sick. Other emails revealed he had organized dance lessons on Valentine's Day, and when he left the house on 14 February without me, I knew exactly what he was up to. *Just get through the pregnancy*, I told myself. *You can't do anything about it right now.*

Emile had driven me to a point where I didn't even recognize myself any more. The woman I used to be would have stuck up for herself, would have got out of a relationship that was so clearly toxic. The woman I was now had no confidence that she could look after herself, let alone her children. His constant lying and the fact I had never dealt with it made me feel weak. His infidelity made me feel totally worthless. What was wrong with me that two husbands had thought so little of me they'd cheated? And every time I raised a concern about his behaviour he turned it back on me, until I felt like it was my fault. I had reached a point where I felt like I was just going through the motions each day for the sake of April. *I'm going to need some help with the baby*, I thought to myself. *I can't just end our marriage now. And if he is prepared to be honest with me, if he admits or explains his behaviour, if he changes, perhaps we could have a future together.* My thoughts went back and forth as I prepared for the new arrival. *I'll give it until our wedding anniversary*, I decided, plucking out the date in six months' time. *If Emile hasn't got any better with me by September then that's the end of it.* I'd had enough.

Just a few days after Valentine's Day, I felt the beginnings of labour pain.

'I think it's happening,' I told my dad over the phone, cradling my stomach.

'OK, Vicky,' he reassured me. 'We're on our way.' I also texted Emile, who told me he'd come straight home after work. I looked over at the time – it was noon. *I guess I'll have to wait it out*, I thought to myself, putting a film on to entertain April. The early stages of labour were slow and uncomfortable. I paced around the living room every so often, waiting for Emile to get home. When he returned from work, followed by my parents who had driven down from Scotland, I decided it was still too soon to go to the hospital.

'I'm fine for now,' I told Emile, who had his head buried in his phone. *Not that you care*, I added to myself. I knew he was keen to go to bed and I didn't have the energy to ask him to stay up with me. 'You may as well go to sleep and I'll wake you when we need to go.'

'OK,' Emile quickly agreed, not needing to be told twice, and I noticed my dad frowning at him.

'Are you sure?' Dad asked me with a worried look on his face, but I nodded.

'You've had a long drive and you need to be rested for April in the morning,' I told him, watching as Emile left the room. 'I'll be fine downstairs on my own.'

'Well, wake us if you need anything,' Dad replied reluctantly, and I smiled. He put his arms around me, giving me a tight hug before heading upstairs. My contractions were still far apart and, in pain, I continued to walk around the room, turning the TV on to distract myself. Restless, I skimmed through a book between pacing and eventually, when the clock showed 1 a.m., I knew I couldn't wait any longer. I carefully carried myself up the stairs to wake Emile.

'It's time to go,' I whispered as I walked into the room, but Emile was already awake. Looking up from his phone, he gave me a small nod.

'OK, let's go.' Emile drove us to the hospital, and by the time we arrived I was quite far gone, but once I was in a delivery suite, labour stalled.

'The baby is stuck,' the midwife informed us, and I knew it was going to be a long night. It took hours before any progress was made, and I had to take a hydro bath to restart labour. Emile sat back in the chair beside my bed, almost silent as I screamed in agony. I was in a fog of pain and drugs and I struggled to stay aware of what was happening around me. A few times I looked over and Emile was holding my hand, but there were periodic moments when I noticed him texting on his phone. I brushed it off and focused on my baby. By the next day, after countless hours of excruciating pain, my cries were matched by a baby's.

'It's a boy,' the midwife congratulated us, placing our baby onto my chest. Bewildered, I peered at my baby boy for the first time.

'Hello,' I cooed. I felt a rush of love as our tiny baby settled down. After a few seconds, I glanced over at Emile who was still slumped in a chair in a corner of the room. My heart sank. *He doesn't seem excited.*

'Do you want to hold him?' I asked, and wordlessly he stood up to take the baby from me. I watched Emile cradle our newborn, rocking him gently in his arms. *He hasn't spoken to me*, I noticed, wishing he would say something. 'Do you love me?' I eventually asked but, still not meeting my gaze, Emile didn't respond. His focus was on the baby, his expression totally blank.

Exhausted, I fell silent again for a while before lifting myself off the bed.

'Can you look after him while I get cleaned up?' I asked, and Emile nodded.

I slowly made my way to the bathroom, suddenly needing a few moments on my own. As soon as I had turned the lock above the handle, I rested my head against the door. *I've just given birth to your baby,* I battled internally, *and you can't even say that you love me.* I was devastated. Stepping into the shower, I turned the tap to let the warm water hit my face, and I started to cry. *I just want to be hugged*, I thought through the tears. *I want to feel loved.* Worn out from the labour and drained from the months of holding everything together on my own, I felt completely worthless.

After a couple of hours, a doctor came to visit us.

'Because of the length of labour,' he told us as I fed the baby, 'there is a risk that the baby could have developed an infection, so we just want to keep you both under observation for twelve hours.'

'OK,' I agreed, nodding.

'You'll be free to head home at about eight o'clock tonight,' the doctor continued.

'That's a bit late,' Emile started to protest, before I could say anything. 'We've got a two-year-old at home.' I lowered my head. *He doesn't want me to come home.*

'Well, Vicky can stay in tonight and go home tomorrow,' the doctor offered. 'Whatever works best for you both.'

'You might as well go home and get some rest.' I

turned to Emile, trying to keep my voice level. 'I'll stay here with the baby and you can pick me up in the morning.' *He doesn't want me so I'll do him a favour and stay here*, I thought to myself bitterly. *At least he doesn't have to bother with me for a night.*

'That's probably best,' Emile agreed and, once the doctor had left the room, he made his excuses to go.

I resigned myself to staying the night in the hospital, but later that afternoon my phone buzzed with an incoming call.

'Listen, I'll come get you tonight,' Emile told me in a change of heart, and I was shocked. 'I think you should be at home.'

'Really?' I felt the excitement in my voice. *That's the first positive thing he has said to me in a long time.*

'Yeah,' Emile continued. 'April is excited to meet her brother. I'll pick you up in a bit.'

'OK,' I replied. 'That's great.'

Emile had allowed April to stay up late to meet her brother and, as we walked through the door, she was beside herself.

'What's he called?' she asked us giddily. Emile and I looked at each other.

'His name is Ben,' I spoke softly to her, beaming at the sight of her cuddling her little brother. I had struggled to pin Emile down to discuss names for the baby. He simply wasn't that interested. On all his documentation in the hospital he was Baby X, which made me feel so sad. I had a shortlist of names that we were both reasonably happy with, but ultimately I made the decision alone.

My parents welcomed me home, taking precious pictures of me with our little bundle of joy. *Maybe things are looking up*, I hoped, noticing Emile putting his arm around me to pose for a photo.

For the first couple of days, life at home with two children felt perfect. Dad and Frances helped out around the house and were welcome company for me while Emile went to work. Even Emile's mood seemed to improve for a while but, once my parents left for Scotland, he went back to his distant self. I remember a postnatal visit from my midwife, who knew me from my pregnancy with April. She could tell something was up, and she managed to get me alone in the kitchen when I broke down in tears: the culmination of trying to keep everything in for days and put up a front that all was well. I dismissed it as the baby blues. I couldn't tell her that my husband was lying to me and cheating on me.

'Vicky,' Emile called, as he headed out of the door one day soon after Ben's birth. 'I'm going to borrow your car for the day.'

'OK,' I started to say, but the front door was already shutting behind him. *What's his problem?* I thought, shaking off the frosty atmosphere. There was nothing wrong with his car, but Emile preferred to use mine and I found that irritating, especially now that I was on maternity leave and could make use of it. The next morning, I got into my car and a waft of stale cigarettes hit me. *Emile has been smoking in my car.* I noticed the ash piled up in the cup holders and immediately I was furious. Jumping out of the car, I stormed back into the house, where Emile was eating his breakfast in the living room.

'You don't have to admit to me or tell me if you're smoking,' I snapped, and Emile looked up in surprise. 'But whatever you do, just do me the courtesy of not smoking in my car.'

'I haven't been smoking in your car,' Emile snapped back in defence, raising his voice over mine. 'How could you accuse me of that.'

'It's not good for me or the children,' I continued, choosing to ignore him. 'And I don't want a car that stinks of smoke.'

'You're accusing me of something I haven't done!' he shouted, jumping up from his seat. The expression on his face was stone-cold, so horrifying I couldn't forget it. His aggressive reaction to what I was saying only confirmed it for me. *You always overreact when you're lying*, I wanted to tell him, but by now I had had enough of his excuses. Not wanting to listen any more, I turned on my heel and left the house. *Stop lying.*

There was no affection between us now. He still helped me out with the children and, at first, he took over the night feed for me once a week, something he had done with April. I was giving Ben his evening feed one Sunday when Emile walked into the bedroom.

'Listen, I'm going to head back to the army barracks tonight,' he told me, grabbing a few of his clothes from the closet.

'Right now?' I looked at the time on my phone. *It's already past ten.* 'It's late.'

'I know,' Emile replied. 'But I can sleep there and that way I'll avoid the traffic in the morning. It just makes sense.' And with that, he left the room. As I finished feeding Ben and placed him back into his cot, I was half listening for the sound of the front door opening and closing. I assumed Emile would first head into the kitchen to make himself a coffee to take with him, as he usually did, but after a while when he was clearly still in the house I wondered what on earth he was doing down there. Eventually I heard him leave.

The next morning, I was the first one awake and, creeping downstairs so as not to wake the kids, I made my way to the kitchen to put the kettle on. Opening the cupboard next to the hob, I reached down to pull out some things for April's lunchbox when I smelt something odd. *Is that gas?* I bent over to peer inside. *Or am I imagining things?* Behind the food was a pipe that fed into the cooker and, taking a deep breath in, I could faintly smell something. *That is definitely gas.* I turned off the lever attached to the pipe, noticing what looked like dried blood along the pipe, and stood up to text Emile. *It could be nothing*, I told myself – my sense of smell had been hyper-sensitive since giving birth. *Did you alter the gas lever in the cupboard? There is dry blood around the lever*, I typed. Emile had cut his hand that weekend and bled copiously – I'd had to clean the counter and cupboard door.

Before long, my phone pinged with a reply from Emile. *That is weird, is the stove working?* I almost laughed.

*I'm not about to try to find out*, I responded, shaking my head. *I'd blow the house up.*

*Open all of the windows and doors and leave it for a while*, he instructed, and so I went through the house, opening up the windows to let the air in. After a while, the smell seemed to have gone so I went back to the pipe and turned the lever on. The reek of gas hit me all at once. Coughing, I turned the pipe off again. *Now what?* I wondered, thinking about the kids asleep upstairs. My phone started ringing on the counter.

'What's happening?' Emile asked as soon as I answered.

'The smell won't go away,' I told him, bending back down to look at the pipe. 'I'm going to have to ring someone.'

'OK, let me know how it goes,' he said, hanging up. Searching for a number online, I called a gasman who arrived that evening.

'It looks like one of the bolts had come loose,' he explained, taking a look at the pipe. 'But I've tightened it up so there should be no problems now.'

'Thank you,' I replied, as he showed me where the pipe had come loose. Out of the blue, a magazine I had read recently suddenly popped into my mind. I thought back to the story inside, where a husband had tried to kill his wife. I smirked, fishing my phone out of my pocket.

*Are you trying to kill me?* I joked in a message to Emile, laughing at the thought.

*Why?* he quickly replied. *You cannot be serious about the comment you've just made, you've been saying that a lot recently. Why would you think that?* I rolled my eyes. *Gosh, he's on the defence*, I thought to myself.

*I read it in a mag recently*, I typed back. *True life stories – my husband tried to kill me.*

*Seriously?* Emile replied and I sighed.

*I was only making a joke because of the blood on the handle, didn't realize I was saying it a lot*, I wrote, before putting my phone away. I racked my brains, trying to think of another time I'd made a similar comment. *I'm sure I haven't*, I thought, but hearing April call me from the living room, I shook my head. Shutting the cupboard door, I tried to push the conversation to the back of my mind and left to attend to my daughter. But as I walked into the living room, I couldn't stop thinking about it. *His reactions are out of control*, I thought to myself. *How could he possibly think I was being serious?*

# 6

# Trapped

Emile's aggressive outbursts were starting to become unbearable.

'Stop checking up on me!' he shouted when I confronted him with yet more proof he was cheating on me. 'I've told you time and time again.'

His abrupt reaction shocked me – it was like an explosion of emotion. *He's so defensive*, I noticed, on edge whenever he went into a fit of rage, but the way he reacted only made me more convinced that he was lying to me. The entire mood of the house was dependent on how Emile was behaving that day. If he was on good form, playing effortlessly with April, our home was a warm mix of squealing children and laughter. On his bad days, however, Emile was irritable, stomping around and acting as if I didn't exist. During these times, the house was quiet and I avoided whichever room he stormed into.

Lying wide awake one night as he snored beside me, I suddenly realized I couldn't take it any more. *I need to get out of here*, I thought. My skin crawled, restless from the stress of living with Emile, and abruptly I sat up. Emile stirred, looking over at me, but I ignored him, rising out of bed to slip on a pair of jeans and a cardigan. We made eye contact for a split-second before he rolled over, turning away from me. Without a second thought, I left our room, making my way across the landing. As I headed down the stairs, the clock in the hallway read 3 a.m. I opened the front door and slammed it hard behind me, making sure Emile would hear. But if he did, he didn't bother to follow me. The frosty March air hit my face as I wandered aimlessly through the streets. *What am I going to do?* I wondered as a helpless, queasy feeling crept into the pit of my stomach. I cast my mind back to my marriage to Liam and, looking back, I winced. *I was too idealistic*, I thought, remembering how soon I had ended things after his affair. *I jumped ship on the marriage too quickly.* It seemed that in my relationship with Emile I was trying to rectify that, but now I felt trapped. The more Emile and I argued about money and his continued lying, the more I just wanted to leave. I was still footing all the bills and had no idea how I was going to pay for both children to be in childcare once I went back to work. *I don't know how much more of this I can take*, I realized, recognizing how drained I was.

Seeking any form of escape, I started to make the most of the early hours of the morning. With the kids in bed and Emile at home, I was free to slip out of the house for a while. Not knowing what to do or who to talk to, I would end up walking for hours through the dark streets, completely distraught, with thoughts rattling around my head as I tried to process what was happening in my marriage. The walks calmed me, but they also made me feel incredibly low because at no point did Emile ever check up on me. There were never any text messages asking where I was or making sure I was all right, although that didn't stop me from pulling out my phone just in case. *He has no compassion for me*, I thought. *He doesn't care.* I didn't want to be at home any more, and would dread the point in my walk where I'd have to turn back. *But I've got the children to think of now*, I would tell myself, slipping quietly back into the house. I had no option but to return. With April and Ben waiting for me, I couldn't just walk away from Emile.

I was so worn down by it all – his cheating and lying, disappearing for weeks on end – that even though the situation was becoming unbearable I still couldn't see any way forward, and I certainly didn't have the strength to tell him to leave. *I do still love Emile, despite everything*, I thought, trying to reassure myself. *And we might come through this, it might be all right. Besides, how can I cope on my own with a newborn?* The persistent idea that things could work out was what kept me going and, for a while, things were just about ticking over at home. With our little boy bringing a new lease of life into the house, Emile seemed to become a bit more attentive, helping out with the night feeds and taking an interest in interacting with Ben. These glimpses of normality gave me hope, and over time life started to look up. Emile began to be more interested in spending time with us, making it home most evenings to sit down with us at dinner. *Maybe we're over the worst*, I let myself believe and, starting to relax, I carried on as if everything was fine. *Maybe things are improving.*

Emile still had his regular mood swings and there were days that I regretted ever having met him, but I clung on to the idea that this was just a rough patch and, one afternoon, my hopes seemed to be confirmed. My phone buzzed on the kitchen counter and I saw that I had an incoming call from Emile.

'You know what I've been thinking?' he said when I picked up the call. He was on his way home from work. 'It would be really good for us to go and jump together.'

My heart leapt. *It's been so long since he's wanted to do anything together*, I smiled, thrilled that he had thought of me. *This is such a positive sign.*

'That would be great,' I said quickly, excited by his sudden interest. 'I'd really like that.'

'Perfect,' Emile replied, and I beamed. 'I'll get in touch with the parachute centre and set it up.' I felt so touched that he'd thought of doing a skydive with me, especially as I hadn't jumped since before falling pregnant with Ben.

'OK, great,' I answered before pausing, suddenly realizing an obvious issue. 'But what are we going to do about the children?'

'We'll sort something out,' he replied. 'I'm sure we can find someone to watch them for twenty minutes.' His tone sounded warm and it was as though I had got the old Emile back. Once he had hung up the phone, I mulled over the prospect of jumping again. It would be my first skydive in a year, and the thought of jumping from a plane filled me with dread. *At least Emile will be with me*, I thought, taking a deep breath. *Maybe this can help get us back on track.*

Since it had been so long since my last jump, a few days later I headed alone to the parachute centre to get my equipment checked over, while Emile stayed home with the kids. *I may as well make sure everything's ready for me to jump*, I thought to myself, knowing the likelihood was that something would need to be fixed. Spotting a friend and parachute colleague, Wez, at reception, I handed over my parachute for him to have a look at.

'Back in a few,' he said, and once he had left, I sat myself down in the foyer to wait. I looked over at the people coming in and out of the centre – it had been so long since I had taught as an instructor that there were many faces I didn't even recognize. *Can I even still do this?* I wondered, petrified at the thought of actually taking a lift and jumping. I snapped back into reality when Wez reappeared with my parachute.

'Your AAD is out of date,' he informed me, and I nodded. I had expected something like this to happen. The automatic activation device was responsible for deploying the reserve parachute if you were going abnormally fast at a low altitude, and without it a jump would be dangerous. 'We'll have to send it to the manufacturer to get it serviced and have the batteries replaced, but this means your parachute and rig will be out of action for the next few weeks.'

'The next few weeks?' I repeated, my heart sinking. 'Emile and I were hoping to do a jump.' I paused before adding, 'Can I rent out some kit?'

'Sure,' he replied, giving me a quick smile. 'It'll be great to have you back.'

At home I filled Emile in on the day's events.

'I'll have to hire kit,' I told him, grabbing some veg from the cupboard as I started to prepare dinner.

'That's good,' he replied, watching me from the kitchen table. He hesitated and I could see he wanted to tell me something.

'What's wrong?' I asked.

'Well,' he started to explain. 'The problem is that I don't think we'll be able to find a sitter.'

'Really?' I asked in slight disbelief, peeling the carrots. 'That's a shame.' *I knew it was too good to be true*, I thought. *Today was a waste of time then*. I should have known Emile would throw a spanner in the works.

'But how about you jump on Saturday and I'll look after the children?' he suggested. At first, I felt deflated. *I thought we were going to jump together*. But I didn't want to upset Emile.

'Perfect,' I replied, turning to face him. 'You can come with me and watch.' Emile gave me a brief smile and I turned my focus back to cooking. I was determined to make the jump a bonding experience.

When Saturday arrived, we bundled the kids into the car. On our way to the centre, I grinned as I listened to April chat away to Emile.

'So Mummy's jumping from high up in the sky?' April asked.

'That's right,' Emile answered, turning round to smile at her. 'And we get to watch.' *He's in a good mood today*, I thought, hoping it would last. I pulled into a space in the airfield car park.

'It's really windy,' I commented, helping Emile take Ben's car seat out of the back. 'Do you reckon they'll even be jumping today?' Looking around at the dismal weather, I had an inkling the flights would be grounded.

'Hopefully,' he shrugged, taking hold of April's hand. 'Let's go find out.' I walked alongside Emile, carrying Ben in his seat, and the four of us made our way to the reception.

'You'll both need to fill out some paperwork for this year,' a member of staff told us. It was the first weekend of April, which meant our annual memberships and checks needed to be renewed. With a stack of papers, we sat down by a coffee table in the foyer and began to work our way through them.

'I need the chief instructor to sign them,' I realized. As an AFF instructor myself, I couldn't fly without his signature to say I was competent to go ahead. 'I'll be right back.' Leaving Emile with the baby, I took hold of April's hand and the two of us wandered off in search of the chief instructor, Mark. When I spotted him outside the offices, I called him over.

'It's been a while since we've seen you,' he said, giving April's hair an affectionate ruffle. 'Are you ready to get back into it?'

'To be honest, I'm not sure if I still want to be an instructor,' I replied. It was a fact I had struggled to admit even to myself, that after so many years of being addicted to the sport, I didn't want to do it any more. 'It's such a massive responsibility,' I added, knowing I would have to be on top of my game the whole time. *I just don't know if I'm going to get back to that point.*

'Well, I'll sign you off for the moment,' he answered, scribbling his signature on the paperwork. 'But we'll support you in whatever decision you make.'

'Thanks,' I replied, grateful for his understanding. Part of the decision-making process for me was to go up on a lift, do a jump and see if I still loved it. I thought back to when I had felt a similar way after giving birth to April. I had been reluctant to continue the sport but when I went up and jumped, I was reminded why I loved it. Skydiving had been like a drug to me but at this stage in life, I felt it could also be quite destructive. Taking April back to the foyer, I considered how damaging it would be to start working here again. There had been times in the past when I had spent entire weekends here, not necessarily jumping or earning any money, just talking to friends, helping students, reading. I should have been spending that time with my husband and April. Emile also did his hobbies at the weekend, still keen on cricket, and it made finding childcare difficult. *Skydiving takes too much time away from my family*, I thought, approaching Emile who was cooing at Ben in the car seat. *I need to focus on that right now.* Once I returned, I picked up Ben in his seat and placed him safely on one of the mats in the centre of the packing hall. With April in tow, Emile and I walked a few feet over to the kit store.

'Ah, I'm not sure I'm allowed to give you that one,' the girl at the kit store remarked. The parachute I had picked was smaller than most, meaning it was fast and I would fall quicker. She called over to Wez to check.

'She's fine to take it out,' he answered. The girl passed the parachute over the counter and Emile picked it up, swinging it over his shoulder by the strap.

'Mummy.' April tugged at my trouser leg as I bought a ticket to jump. 'I need to go to the toilet.'

'OK, sweetheart,' I replied, glancing over at Ben in his seat. 'Just a second.'

'No, I'll take her,' Emile interjected, taking April's hand.

'Sure,' I answered, grateful for the offer. I watched them head off towards the toilet. *I'd only struggle getting her to cooperate.* April was a daddy's girl through and through. Leaving Emile to take her, I went back over to the mats and scooped Ben up into my arms, cradling him as I waited for them to return. Watching as people walked past, I kept catching the eyes of other jumpers who I vaguely knew.

'Hi,' I nodded awkwardly as they passed. I felt uncomfortable, making small talk with a few of the people I spotted. *I don't really know anyone here any more*, I realized. I looked down at my watch, willing Emile to rescue me from the awkward social interactions.

'What's taking them so long?' I muttered to Ben, when April and Emile still hadn't returned. Picking up my son, I walked over to the toilets. There was one door, which led to three more: the women's, men's and a shower room. I pushed open the first door and immediately heard April chattering away to Emile in one of the toilets. *They're fine*, I realized, and I went back to my spot by reception. I wasn't sure how long they had been gone – it could have been five minutes, it could have been ten minutes – but shortly after I sat back down, Emile and April followed out of the toilets. Emile came to sit beside me on the mats.

'Hello,' he cooed to Ben, who was gurgling away on the floor, and April plonked herself down on my lap. I noticed an instructor walking towards us.

'There are no lifts right now,' he told me. 'The weather's taken a bit of a turn.'

'OK,' I replied. *What a waste of time*. April was struggling in my arms, getting restless.

'It's past her dinner time,' I said to Emile, checking my watch. 'I doubt I'm going to fly today – shall we just go home?' I could tell Ben was starting to get hungry and I didn't see the point in staying any longer.

'I suppose,' Emile agreed reluctantly. 'Just seems a shame.'

'I'll come back another day,' I replied, getting Ben settled back into his car seat. 'The weather will have picked up in a couple days.' I glanced at the parachute still sitting over Emile's shoulder. 'We need to return the kit,' I added. I looked over at the kit store, but there was no one at the counter. Emile followed my gaze.

'Just leave it in your locker,' he shrugged, scooping April into his arms. 'You need to sort stuff out in there anyway.' Emile was right, it had been months since I had last checked the equipment in my locker.

'I guess they won't mind,' I answered, getting ready to leave. 'It could take us ages to find someone now.'

The kids were growing increasingly restless and, fearing a full-scale meltdown in the centre, I followed Emile down the corridor to my locker. Keeping the parachute overnight wasn't something I would normally do, and by no means was I meant to, but the weather seemed too dismal for anyone to need the kit. Taking the parachute from him, I stowed it in the locker.

'Just do the jump tomorrow,' Emile said, and I nodded. Tomorrow was set to be a busy day, with my first social outing since giving birth planned for the afternoon. *Even if I don't get a chance to jump, I'll come back anyway to return the kit*, I decided. The parachute centre knew me, I worked there – they could call me if it became an issue.

Once home, I fed the children and settled into an ordinary evening. Emile bathed April while I settled Ben down in his cot.

'Please sleep tonight,' I whispered, stroking his hair. My friend Alex was hosting a barbecue for her partner's birthday the following afternoon, and I wanted to use this evening to express milk so I could have a few drinks at the party. Once I had settled Ben, I headed back downstairs, where Emile was watching TV in the living room. I perched myself beside him.

'What do you want to watch?' he asked, flicking through the channels with the remote. He placed a hand affectionately on my leg and I almost jolted in shock. I glanced over but he was still gazing at the TV. *Things really are looking up*, I thought. A small smile was etched across my face.

'We can watch whatever,' I replied, relaxing my back on the sofa. The house was no warmer than any other night but tonight it felt cosy. I thought about my babies asleep upstairs and I almost wanted to cry. *My perfect family.*

# 7

# The Jump

Nervous at the prospect of the looming jump, I had hoped Ben would sleep through the night but no matter what I did, I just couldn't get him to settle down. He wailed relentlessly, and periodically throughout the early hours I was jolted awake, rushing over to his cot to attend to him. *Maybe this is a sign*, I thought, rocking him gently in my arms. *Perhaps I shouldn't go through with it.* By the time morning rolled around, I had barely had a couple of hours of sleep and I was utterly exhausted. With the sun peeking through the curtains, I finally got Ben settled to the point where I thought he was going to sleep. *Thank god for that*, I thought to myself, creeping out of the room at the first chance I got. Completely drained, I dragged myself downstairs and into the kitchen, where I put the kettle on. After a couple of minutes, Emile joined me, pouring himself a cup of tea.

'I don't know if I'll have time any more,' I said to him as he took a seat across from me at the table. 'Ben hasn't stopped crying all night.'

'Well, why don't you just pop out now and do the

jump while he's asleep?' Emile suggested as I slumped over my morning coffee. 'That way you can come back and get ready for the party.'

'I suppose you're right,' I agreed reluctantly, glancing at the clock. 'I should probably just get it out of the way.' The jump had been playing so much on my mind and I knew that if I could just get it over and done with, I could stop worrying and enjoy myself in the afternoon. With the decision made, I finished my coffee and left, giving April a tight squeeze before heading out of the door. For the entire drive to the parachute centre, I felt sick with nerves. After an awful night's sleep and with the party to prepare for, it didn't feel right to tear myself away. I wished for all the world that Emile could be here to jump beside me, and I hated the thought of going alone. *But Emile's planned this for me*, I thought to myself. *I have to see it through*.

By the time I arrived at the parachute centre, it was late morning and the sky was overcast. I gave myself a few minutes to sit in the car, taking in the view of the airfield. *Come on, Vicky.* I took a deep breath and opened the car door. *The sooner I go, the sooner I can come back*. I headed into the building and made a bee-line for the locker where Emile had left my parachute. Taking all of my kit out and checking over the rented parachute, I made my way to the hangar. I was surprised by how quickly I was called to the flight line. After only waiting for ten minutes, I was summoned to the plane with a few other jumpers, where we were checked over and given the OK to fly.

'You're good to go,' an instructor confirmed, after making sure all of my kit was in place. He gave me the thumbs-up and I joined the queue to board the plane. I waited anxiously – seeing the aircraft for the first time made my legs shake with nerves – but no sooner was I about to get on the plane when I was called back.

'Everyone, stand down,' another instructor came out to tell us. 'Come back to the hangar. The morning lift has been called off due to the weather, so you'll have to go back inside and wait.' Amongst the groans from other jumpers that followed, I felt a flutter of relief. *Good*, I thought to myself. I didn't know why, and it felt too irrational to articulate to anyone else, but I had a terrible feeling about the jump. It was like a sixth sense: something inside me was screaming not to do it. I marched with everyone else back into the hangar, where I took my kit off, hanging my parachute up on one of the hooks.

*The weather is too bad for a jump*, I wrote in a text to Emile. *Don't think it's going to happen.*

*Hopefully it will pick up soon*, he replied. *Stay for a bit and see if you can get on a lift later.* I set my phone aside and lay down on one of the mats used as makeshift beds. *I may as well get some sleep while I can*, I decided, not taking for granted the rare moment I had without a toddler and a baby to attend to. I waited and waited for the weather to pick up, but as the morning wore into afternoon, I had begun to give up hope.

*How are things at home with the kids?* I asked Emile, bored of being at the parachute centre.

*Fine*, he typed back. *Ben's made his way through most of the milk.*

*Already?* I replied, slightly annoyed. I had expressed that milk specifically for tonight's party, but with me at the airfield, I'd had no choice but to instruct Emile to use it. I went back to the car to retrieve my breast pump. It had now gone beyond the few hours that I'd normally feed Ben and the pain was becoming unbearable. *If I can't jump today then at least Ben can eat this tonight*, I thought, taking refuge in an empty shower room to express milk. Rubbing my hands along my temple, I could feel myself getting restless. *This is a waste of time*, I thought, digging my phone out of my pocket.

*Maybe I should just come home*, I typed to Emile. *Then I can spend some time with the kids and still have enough time to get ready.*

*No, you should stay*, Emile wrote back, and I sighed. *Maybe he's saying that because he knows how nervous I am*, I considered. It had been so long since my last jump that it felt almost alien to me now.

*It says online that the weather should be clearing up soon*, another message from Emile read.

*He seems to really care about this*, I thought, seeing how much of an interest Emile was taking. *I can't give up now.* I knew that if I didn't jump now it could be months before I would get another chance. Collecting my things, I started to make my way back into the hangar, wrapping the milk and pump under my coat in an effort to be discreet. As a result, I ended up spilling the milk over my coat.

'For god's sake,' I muttered, cross with myself. *As if this day couldn't get any worse.* I felt fed up. *I just want to be at home with my babies*, I moaned internally. With more texts of encouragement from Emile, I stayed and waited, and eventually, after what felt like forever, I got the call.

'We're doing a low-level lift,' one of the instructors told everyone waiting in the hangar. 'A hop and pop.' I breathed a slight sigh of relief. A low-level jump meant the plane would only be flying up to the cloud base, reaching 5,000 feet at most. *I can do this*, I thought. *A hop and pop is easy.* I held my nerve, getting my kit together before boarding the plane, but as soon as I sat down, I felt a wave of regret. *I don't want to be here*, I realized, wishing I could just stand up and run out of the plane. I couldn't figure out why, but everything seemed wrong and that niggling feeling of a sixth sense came creeping back into my mind. *I shouldn't be here, I should be at home.* I was sitting right behind the pilot and, with everyone else sitting facing the tail, no one could see the tears welling in the corners of my eyes. Yet I lifted my helmet over my head and fitted it into place, hiding my eyes behind the visor. I started to shake, closing my eyes for fear of throwing up. I was an experienced jumper so I knew no one was going to pay particular attention to me, but I had a nauseating feeling of dread as the plane engine revved and took off for the sky. I was scared, more so than I had been for any other jump. I thought about the children, about five-week-old Ben waiting for me at home. Today was the first time I'd had any real separation from him, and the hormonal pull I felt made me feel awful. *I just need to get the jump over with and go home*, I thought to myself, resolving already that this would be my final jump. Ignoring my irrational worries, I tried to focus on what was happening, listening to the pilot as he shouted over to us.

'The clouds are lower than we expected,' the pilot called out. 'And the jump master has made the decision that only a few people can exit with each pass.'

I groaned at the news, realizing as I sat at the back that I would have to wait for everyone else to jump before I could. When the time came, the first person got up and lifted the plane door open. Instantly, the entire aircraft was engulfed by noise. A few seconds went by before he jumped, disappearing into the sky below us. The plane looped the airfield three times, and with each pass more jumpers exited the aircraft, until finally it was my turn. Once I was alone, I felt myself kick into gear, letting my fears be pushed to the back of my mind. I had jumped so many times before and this part felt like second nature. I knelt up from the floor, heading for the tail of the plane, and crouched over the open door. I stared down at the earth 3,000 feet below, waiting until I could see the field below me. I paused. Then I was given the signal to go, and I held my breath and leapt into the sky.

A rush of cold air hit my face as I fell from the plane. For the first time all day, I felt calm. *I know what I'm doing.* With ease, I spread my arms out in front of me, navigating myself through the air with careful control. I reached for the toggle at the base of the rig strapped to my back and pulled it outwards, deploying the parachute. The canopy billowed out above but instead of slowing me down, I felt an uneven jolt. *That's weird*, I thought, looking up at the parachute. Examining the ropes, I could see that the lines attached to the parachute were badly twisted. For a split-second I was in shock, but I snapped myself out of it. *I've seen this before*, I told myself, annoyed by what appeared to be a common problem. *This is nothing I can't get out of.* When you have done as many jumps as I had, it was almost guaranteed I would have encountered a few problems before.

My training had taught me to kick through the air, unravelling the twists as I went. *It's working*, I thought, seeing the lines begin to untangle. But then it became clear that something wasn't right as I peered up at the useless parachute above me. I tried in vain to figure out what was wrong but none of my years as a free-fall instructor could have prepared me for whatever was happening. *I can't fix it*, I recognized, understanding that there was no way I'd be able to work out why the main parachute wasn't cooperating. *No one will blame me for using the reserve.* I had to act fast, cutting away my parachute as I dropped further through the sky. I held my breath, preparing myself for what would be an aggressive jolt from the fast-acting back-up. I tugged another toggle to open the reserve parachute and closed my eyes.

The reserve was designed to open instantly, in a snap motion that would make you jerk upwards. I waited for it, the sharp tug upwards indicating that the reserve was deployed, but I felt nothing. Opening my eyes, I looked up in horror. The reserve canopy had only partially inflated, with one side flapping uselessly in the wind. The malfunction caused the parachute to begin to spin out of control. *Shit*, I panicked. *This is just my luck.* Where I should have been upright with the parachute above me, the violent spins were knocking me sideways, until I was almost upside down. *How the hell am I going to get out of this?* I fought against the elements, tugging desperately on the risers above my head. I kicked my legs in the opposite direction, struggling against the wind. Trying to free the lines in any way I could, I pushed against the way they were twisted. They didn't budge at first, but once I got the momentum going, kicking with everything I had, the lines started to untangle. *Thank god*, I thought as I slowly tilted upright, but any initial relief I felt was short-lived. As soon as the lines had unravelled, I began to spin even more violently. The canopy threw me around in a dizzy haze as I tugged tirelessly at the risers, trying everything I could to take control of my accelerating plunge. I had no idea how close I was to the ground, my gaze solely focused on the failing parachute above me.

*The children need me*, I thought, panic sparking as nothing seemed to work. *I need to sort this shit out.* I stared at the lines. *I have to slow down.* For the life of me, I couldn't work out what was wrong. *If I can just figure out what's happening, I can fix it*, I thought over the scream of the air. The furious spinning was creating what I knew to be a centrifugal force effect, but as I tumbled further down, I couldn't work out the cause. *It's supposed to be a docile canopy, how can this be happening?* I thought. *This can't be happening.* But I pushed any fear from my mind. *I just have to fix it*, I told myself, letting my mind slip into autopilot. *There's no other option.* With only half of the canopy working, I pulled as hard as I could to bring my speed down, struggling against the outrageous rate I was falling at. I plummeted in a violent spin through the sky, fighting for the parachute to cooperate, fighting for my life. Out of nowhere, there was a loud metallic bang. Then everything went black.

# 8

# Surviving

Slowly coming round, before I even opened my eyes, the first thing that hit me was the smell in the air. *Is that dirt?* I tentatively felt the soft ground underneath me, clutching at the soil. *I'm still alive.* I moved my fingers slightly and then my toes, and when both responded, I breathed a sigh of relief. *Everything works*, I thought to myself. *I'm on the ground and everything works.* Dizzy from the fall, I carefully opened my eyes, squinting under the sunlight.

'Oh thank god, Vicky!' someone exclaimed, and I recognized the woman kneeling over me as a friend from the parachute centre, Kate. *She's a trained doctor*, I remembered in silence, watching her as she checked me over. I was aware of a blur of people surrounding me, with worried expressions etched across their faces. The blaring noise of an ambulance grew louder in the distance. The world turned fuzzy and everything went black again. The next time I opened my eyes, I was fixed to a stretcher. A whirring sound screeched above me and, with my head in a brace, I could just about make out the roof above. *Am*

*I in a helicopter?* I wondered, realizing the loud sound came from the helicopter rotor flying us above Wiltshire. Again, I wiggled my fingers and, content they could work, I wiggled my toes. *Everything's fine.*

'Oh,' the paramedic beside me said, noticing I was awake. 'Hello there, we're just about to land at Southampton.' He peered over my stretcher, offering a smile.

'Southampton?' I croaked in confusion. 'Why am I not just going to Salisbury?' I knew the latter hospital was much closer than Southampton and, lying in a daze as we flew through the air, I felt embarrassed at so much effort and expense just for me. *This is all so unnecessary.*

'Southampton has the major trauma unit,' the paramedic answered. 'That's why we need to go there.' *This is some serious overkill*, I thought. *I've done the checks and I'm not in any pain, I'm absolutely fine.* I couldn't figure out what all of the fuss was about, but suddenly I was sleepy again and, unable to fight it, I drifted off.

When I awoke I was still on my stretcher, but now I was being wheeled into A&E. My mind felt numb and everything around me seemed surreal. *Are all of these doctors really here for me?* I asked myself, taking in my surroundings. My skydiving kit had been removed, and peering down I saw the hospital gown I had been dressed in. There was a lot of conversation happening above me, with different doctors whizzing past to check my IV drip and delegate jobs to other members of staff. I drifted in and out of consciousness, fighting to keep my eyes open as hospital staff fussed over me. *What is happening?* I tried to ask, but no words came out of my mouth. Unable to stay awake any longer, I let the world fade to black again, and all of the chaos and noise died down into silence.

By the time I was able to open my eyes properly, my stretcher had been replaced by a small hospital bed and I was lying in the centre of a large room in A&E. Emile was by my side, slouched in a chair.

'Hi,' I croaked and he looked up, a small smile appearing on his face for a split-second.

'Finally, you're awake,' he replied, with no hint of emotion in his tone. He didn't bother to rise from his seat. 'How are you feeling?'

'Um.' I hesitated, wiggling my fingers and toes once more for good measure. 'Fine.'

'Good,' Emile answered, gazing around at the busy hospital staff rushing past us. 'We've been here for quite a while, you know.'

'I'm so sorry,' I quickly apologized, feeling the guilt rise in my stomach. 'I didn't mean to cause all of this hassle.'

'It's fine,' Emile told me, yet I couldn't help but notice that he didn't disagree that this was my fault. *God, he's going to like me even less now*, I thought, angry with myself for the parachute accident. *I'm causing all of these problems*. The rational part of my mind knew I hadn't done anything wrong. It was impossible for any of this to be my fault, but I couldn't stop myself from feeling that I was to blame. My head was spinning from whatever drugs had been given to me, and seeing the faces fly past the end of my bed in a blur was making me feel sick. I closed my eyes, trying to block out the noise ringing in my ears.

'Hi Victoria,' I heard someone say, and I jumped, snapping my eyes open. A nurse had approached the side of my bed. 'We're going to take you for a CT scan now.'

'OK,' I slurred. 'That's fine.'

'We're just going to top up your ketamine,' she informed me, moving to the IV attached to my arm. *They're giving me ketamine?* I thought as another nurse joined to wheel me out of the room. *That's a bit extreme.* Amidst the fog of drugs and confusion, I couldn't understand why all of this was happening but, before I knew it, the top-up to my painkillers began to take effect. The room fell quiet as the world closed in on me and I was unconscious again.

When I finally came round, I was back in the make-shift room at A&E and it felt as though I had never left.

'How are you feeling, Victoria?' a doctor asked, noticing I had woken up.

'OK, I think,' I answered, unsure of what else to say. 'I'm not in any pain.'

'That's good to hear,' he replied. 'You're on very strong medication right now so there shouldn't be any pain.' Struggling to take in what the doctor was saying,

I looked at all of the faces around my bed and amongst them I spotted Emile.

'I've called your parents,' he told me, catching my eye. 'They're coming.' There was a comforting tone to his voice but the news only made me feel worse. *My poor parents*, I worried. *Having to come all this way.*

'Why have you called them?' I asked, feeling like I could cry. 'I'm fine, there's no need.' There were a lot of staff moving around my bed, sorting out the various machines around me. The window by Emile suggested it was the start of early evening, with daylight dimming behind him.

'Vicky, you've had quite a bad fall,' he replied, before fishing his phone from his pocket. 'Do you want to talk to them?' Before I could answer, Emile placed the handset to my ear and I listened to the dial tone.

'Hello?' Dad answered, and I could tell it was from the speakerphone in his car.

'Hi Dad, it's Victoria,' I said, my voice still croaky.

'Oh my god, Victoria,' Dad replied, sounding strained. 'We've been so worried. Are you all right?'

'Yeah, I'm fine,' I told him, struggling to speak. 'I'm in hospital and they're just doing some tests.'

'OK,' he told me. 'We're heading to the house and we'll come down to the hospital to see you tomorrow.'

'Sure,' I said, letting out a sigh. The promise of seeing my parents was a sudden comfort.

'I'm so glad you're OK,' my dad continued, and his voice seemed to crack as he spoke.

'I am, Dad,' I tried to reassure him. 'I'll talk to you later.' When the call clicked off, Emile put the phone back in his pocket.

'The kids are with Carly right now,' Emile informed me. 'But your parents are going to take them when they get here.' I nodded. *That's really nice of his ex-wife*, I thought to myself. *To look after April and Ben.* The demands of a five-week-old breastfed baby were not lost on me. We used to see Emile's children from his first marriage often at weekends and then, as he got busier, as and when he could. They got on well with April and I was keen that they grew up in each other's lives. Emile dealt with the practicalities of the visits with Carly so I didn't often see her, but I had no issues with her. She was a single mother doing her best to bring up her children.

'Have you got Ben some formula?' I asked, suddenly realizing I would no longer be able to feed him.

'Yes, I took some round to her,' Emile replied, giving me a brief smile before appearing stoic again. 'Both kids are fine.'

I breathed a slight sigh of relief, but knowing Ben would now have to be bottle-fed became yet another piece of guilt to add to my list. *I've messed things up for everyone*, I thought. *I can't even care for my baby.* The overwhelming sense of worthlessness was ever growing.

'Hello Victoria.' One of the consultants entered the room, interrupting my thoughts. 'How are you doing?'

'OK,' I shrugged, watching him from my bed as he flipped through my notes.

'Well, I think it's safe to say that you have broken your pelvis,' he replied. 'We've given you a pelvic binder to hold everything together until we can operate.'

'I see,' I answered, taking in what the consultant was telling me. I looked down and noticed for the first time that there was a band strapped around my waist.

'I have a colleague who has an interest in pelvic trauma, he's going to come in tomorrow and do the surgery,' he continued. 'He'll get it fixed for you.'

'Sounds great,' I replied. I still hadn't experienced any pain and it was hard to imagine I'd actually broke something, but peering back down at the pelvic binder fastened around my hips, I began to comprehend that I must have done some damage in the fall. After another hour of waiting, a nurse came by to adjust it.

'I think it's a bit too tight,' he commented, pointing to the binder. 'I'm just going to loosen it.' Wordlessly, I watched him reach for the straps that kept the band tight against my torso and began to untie them.

'Ah!' I screamed in agony and shock. 'What the hell!' Pain shot through my pelvis and it felt as if my body was going to rip in two. As quickly as he had loosened it, he tightened it up again and the excruciating pain suddenly faded. I panted for breath, horrified by what had just happened.

'We'll just keep it tightened for now then,' the nurse said in a hurry, giving me a small, apologetic smile before leaving the room. I couldn't believe the pain I had just felt. *How hurt am I?* I wondered in a panic. I clearly had not appreciated just how much the painkillers were masking my injuries. I looked over at Emile, who seemed engrossed in his phone.

'What's going on now then?' I asked abruptly, annoyed that he wasn't paying attention to what was happening with me. I was aware it had now been several hours since the fall and the kids would be wondering where I was. He glanced up from the screen, taking a couple of seconds to answer.

'I'll go and find out,' he replied, clambering out of his chair to go in search of a doctor. Alone and strapped to the bed, I felt helpless. I closed my eyes, counting down the seconds until he returned with a nurse. It felt like it took an eternity.

'We're just waiting for a bed to become available on intensive care,' the nurse explained to me while Emile fell back into his seat. 'And then we can get you settled.'

Once again, I couldn't help but think this was an over-reaction. *Yes, I've got a broken pelvis but I'm not dying. It's just a broken bone.* It may have been the blissful high I was feeling from the drugs or the fact that I hadn't processed the information properly, but it wasn't until another doctor arrived to see me and explained the true extent of the damage the fall had caused that I accepted just how injured I was.

'You have a broken pelvis, yes,' the doctor repeated, looking through my notes. 'But we think that may have damaged your bladder too. You've also broken most of the ribs along your right side and part of your right lung has collapsed.'

'What?' I asked out loud in disbelief. The details were shocking.

'You're very lucky to be alive,' he continued, and those words stayed with me. 'Right now, we don't know if you have an unstable spinal fracture, so we're going to put you on full spinal care to protect your spinal cord.'

Lying flat on my back, I fell silent, taking in the news. I thought about April and Ben waiting for me at home. *I almost lost everything*, I realized, and the hairs on the back of my neck rose, my skin tingling with horror. I peered over to Emile, who was still sitting by my side, but the bored expression on his face was obvious. *Give me a kiss and a hug*, I pleaded internally. *Tell me you love me*. But he didn't move. I watched in silence while one of the nurses checked the IV fitted into my arm.

'We need to get you off this bed and onto a trolley,' she told me. I looked around – getting off the hospital bed looked impossible. 'I'm not going to sugar-coat it,' the nurse continued. 'It's going to hurt but you can do it.'

'OK,' I agreed, taking a deep breath. *Just get me out of A&E*, I added to myself, exhausted from the day. *I'm not in any pain anyway*. There were five staff standing around the bed, ready to roll me onto the trolley.

'Are you ready?' one of them asked, and I nodded. In one motion, they began to move me.

'Ah!' I screamed. 'No, stop!' The second I moved even slightly to the side, my whole body was in flames.

'We've got to do this,' the doctor persisted. It took everything I had not to resist. It was excruciating. They laid me down flat on the A&E trolley and I sobbed, traumatized by what had just happened. *I have never felt anything that horrific*, I thought, tears streaming down my face.

'Well done, you did it,' the doctor tried to reassure me. 'Now let's get you to your ward.'

Emile followed as I was wheeled through the hospital, taking the large elevator up to the intensive care unit. As we approached my spot on the ward, I looked with horror at what I was being wheeled towards – *another bed*.

'No, please,' I begged, feeling sick as the doctors positioned me beside the bed. 'I can't do it, just leave me on this.' The thought of having to go through that degree of pain again, being rolled on broken ribs and a broken pelvis, was too much to bear.

'I'm sorry,' they sympathized, letting the sides of the trolley fold down. 'But we've got to get you onto the bed, and the only way to do that safely is with a log roll.'

I screamed as they moved me from the trolley. I couldn't stop myself, I sounded like a wild animal. Emile looked on in silence, watching me in the worst agony I had ever been in. The noises I made didn't even sound like me, they were yelled in utter desperation. Once in the bed, I lay in shock, holding my breath until the pain subsided.

'The worst is over,' the doctor reassured me, giving my shoulder a sympathetic pat. The lack of attention from Emile was blazingly obvious. He held back, lingering behind the doctors with his beloved mobile phone in his hand. *He could at least pretend.* I was embarrassed by how blatant his disinterest was. Over the course of the next day, Emile did all of the functional things that were required of him. He made sure the house was ticking over, that April and Ben were happy and cared for. Whatever I asked for, he brought to me, but not a shred of emotion seemed to escape, and it was the emotional support that I really needed.

Dad and Frances arrived the next morning to visit me in hospital, and the look on my dad's face when he saw for himself what state I was in was heartbreaking. He wiped the tears from his eyes, trying to put on a brave expression. Dad did his best to hide what was happening back at home, but from the strained silences, I could tell tensions were growing between him and Emile. *There's nothing I can do about it*, I decided, choosing to ignore the atmosphere. I hated being trapped in the hospital and how out of control I was over my own life. While Dad and Frances were there, I was taken down for surgery on my pelvis. The operation lasted three or four hours, during which the surgeon put my pelvis back together like a jigsaw, the pieces held in place with some of the NHS's finest hardware. After that, I was left to recover in intensive care. Stuck on the hospital ward with nowhere to go, I felt completely lost.

'I just want to see my babies,' I cried to a consultant who was making her rounds.

'I know you do, Vicky,' she replied softly. 'But you know it's just not safe to have them here.' It hurt like hell to hear, but I knew she was right. I spoke at length with the various doctors who came to see me, asking them about the possibility of April and Ben coming into the ward.

'There are some nasty bugs floating around the ICU,' one of the doctors confirmed for me. 'And with your youngest not even having had his injections yet, the risks are just too high.' I nodded in agreement.

'It's for the best,' I replied, not wanting anything bad to happen to my two children. Even so, the separation from them ate away at me and I cried to Emile, longing to go home.

'I miss them,' I sobbed, feeling helpless. 'I just want them here with me.'

'OK,' Emile replied. 'I'll see what I can do.' As I started to regain some strength, Emile set it up so that I could use my phone to FaceTime with April.

'Hi darling,' I smiled, waving at her happy face on the screen.

'Mummy!' she exclaimed, chattering half-nonsense to me down the phone. I watched her carry me around the house, showing off her favourite toys onscreen.

'That looks fun,' I chimed. April giggled and I beamed. Emile brought in some story books from her collection and every evening, I read to her. Whenever he could, Dad showed Ben to me on the phone and I teared up, seeing how even in the space of a few days, he had changed.

'I just want to get home to him,' I cried, my heart breaking every time I saw his face.

'I know you do,' Dad replied, and I could tell how much seeing me upset was hurting him. 'April and Ben are both absolutely fine and we know you'll be home in no time.' *I have to be*, I thought. *I just have to get better.* I was restless in the hospital bed and lying flat on my back was unbearable. Every few hours, the pain would heighten and I'd beg to be moved.

'Please just roll me,' I implored an intensive care nurse. It took a five-man log roll to move me onto my good side, releasing the pressure that had built up from being flat on my back. After each roll, I tried my hardest to last longer before complaining again, but every three hours I would find myself begging to be moved again.

Meanwhile, I found the hospital to be terribly lonely. Friends would visit me as often as they could, but Emile was rarely there. He insisted he hadn't been allowed any time off work and, while I found that excruciatingly hard to believe, I just didn't have the energy to fight him on it. When he went home from work each night to relieve Dad and Frances of their childminding duties, the pair would drive to the hospital to spend the evening with me. I spent each day looking forward to them coming, anxious to hear how April and Ben were doing. I accepted the fact that Emile didn't visit me. *It's what's best for the children*, I told myself, glad that they still had the continuity of at least one parent being home. Really, though, I just wanted Emile by my side. Without a break from the mind-numbing boredom, each day in hospital dragged. I had a button by my bedside that when pressed would administer a powerful painkiller, Fentanyl, through my IV, and I used it to forget where I was. I would be floating on a cloud somewhere, happy and safe. On the odd occasion that Emile did appear, the nursing staff were quick to tell him he was allowed in whenever he wanted.

'We totally understand that you have kids,' one nurse said, trying to help. 'You can come any time, you don't have to stick to visiting hours.'

'Thanks,' Emile replied, but he never took them up on their offer. *How humiliating*, I thought. *Everyone must know he doesn't really care.* I knew the family and friends who supported me were starting to pick up on Emile's blasé attitude and I was deeply embarrassed.

'If that was my wife, I'd be off work for weeks,' one friend commented. 'I'd be in hospital as much as I could.' I blushed but I couldn't deny they were right. Emile's attitude towards me didn't make sense. *People deal with things in different ways*, I tried to tell myself, but I couldn't help but feel let down by him. I felt so alone and, whilst grieving at the sudden separation from my baby, sometimes it felt like I was also grieving for my marriage. *He's just not there*, I noted, watching the vacant expression on Emile's face. The only thing that kept me going was the thought of April and Ben. I was determined to recover and get home to my babies as fast as possible, but the consultants in the unit were concerned about a burst fracture in my spine, which looked as if a little firework had gone off inside my T8 vertebra. A fragment was right by my spinal cord. (I'd also broken three lumbar vertebrae but the doctors were less concerned by those.)

'It's potentially an unstable fracture,' a spinal surgeon who arrived to check me over said. 'Which means it's likely you'll be in hospital for about three months while we assess it.' The comment floored me.

'That's not possible,' I responded, shaking my head. 'What are the alternatives?'

'Well, in theory we could operate,' he replied. 'But I'm reluctant to.'

I thought about my options. *I'm not going to get into a much worse situation*, I decided. *I'm already in intensive care as it is, so I may as well push on with the surgeries.*

'I want the surgery,' I told him, but he didn't seem keen.

'I'll reassess and get back to you,' he replied and, much to my frustration, he left it at that. I spent the next few days nagging to see him, asking any consultant who checked me to send for him. Eventually, he spoke to Emile.

'He talked to you?' I asked in disbelief. *How could he talk to Emile about it and not me?*

'He doesn't want to do the surgery,' Emile shrugged. I

was furious and when the ICU consultant did her rounds, I made a point to tell her exactly how I felt.

'Emile's not medically trained – I am,' I vented, frustrated that my opinion hadn't been taken into consideration. 'It's my body, for god's sake.'

'Well,' the consultant replied as she flicked through my chart, 'you are well within your rights to seek a second opinion.'

'That would be great,' I said, eager for anyone to listen to what I wanted. 'Can you get someone for me?'

'Absolutely,' she agreed, and the next day another spinal surgeon came to see me.

'We first need to assess whether or not your spine is stable,' he told me, and it was a relief to have someone take me seriously. 'The only way to do that is to get you upright in a brace and do some weight-bearing x-rays. That will help us to see what happens to the vertebrae in the spine.' He explained that the burst vertebra would either press down and was therefore unstable, or it wouldn't, meaning it was stable. 'If it presses down then I'm more than happy to surgically stabilize it for you.' I smiled. His whole manner impressed me, and the fact that he spoke to me at length on the issue felt like all the reassurance I needed.

'Let's do it,' I agreed, eager to be on the mend. I had already searched for this surgeon on Google before he had arrived. *He's ex-military*, I remembered, and I found that fact to be a comfort.

'Well, first,' he interrupted, gazing over at the drip

attached to my arm, 'we need to address your drug addiction.' I followed his stare to the IV pumping me with a powerful dose of painkillers. I had barely felt any pain the whole time I had been in ICU, but now that I had been moved to a ward, it was time to wean myself off it.

'I see,' I replied, finding yet another obstacle between me and home.

'I'll give you the back brace when you come off the Fentanyl,' he promised, and I agreed. Shortly after the surgeon had left, I had a nurse come and remove the drug altogether. *I'll just stop taking it now*, I decided. *Whatever it takes to get myself out of here*. I swapped the IV for tablets to help with my pain management and, the next morning, a brace was delivered to my bed.

'Shall we try it on?' the physio asked me. After years of treating other people with physiotherapy, it was bizarre to be treated myself. I shifted slightly as the physio fitted the brace around my torso, tightening it at the front. Two physios helped me log roll and start to elevate myself. 'When you're ready, sit up.' I lifted myself off the bed, managing to sit up at about a forty-five-degree angle, and immediately felt sick. It had been a week and a half since I'd arrived in the ICU and, after spending all of that time lying flat on my back, my body had been retrained to find that normal. Sitting up now seemed impossible.

'This is a hideous feeling,' I muttered, groaning at the dizziness I felt. 'It's like a magnified version of the worst hangover ever.' I managed about two minutes upright before needing to lie back down. *I have to last long enough to have an x-ray*, I realized. *I have to be able to stand up.*

'Can you leave me with the back brace on?' I asked, and the physio nodded. After that, each time the clock hit the hour I forced myself to sit up, watching how long I could last. *That was three minutes*, I thought, lying back on the bed. *Next time, I'll stay up for longer.* The nausea I felt when upright didn't go away but I distracted myself, playing on my phone or looking around the room, trying to ignore how awful it was. It helped that I had some medical knowledge behind me. I didn't need telling to keep my joints moving. I did routine exercises from my bed, moving my hips and practising my breathing. *I'm not going to burden anyone else with the task of getting me better*, I decided. *I'm going to do it myself.* By the time I was due to go for my x-ray the next day, I was able to swing my legs to the side of the bed and, slowly, stand up.

'I can't believe it,' the spinal surgeon commented, watching in awe as I shuffled towards him. 'There's nothing you can't do.'

I let myself smile. It took me forever to stabilize myself on the ground, and standing upright I endured the pain long enough only to have my x-ray done, but I did it. *I'll walk myself home if I have to*, I mused. *Whatever it takes to get back to my babies.*

I had half hoped Emile would appear to show some

support but, in the end, he was nowhere to be seen. *Is it really a surprise?* I asked myself. I had been alone throughout my second pregnancy and the entire time he had been abroad. When I had plummeted to the ground, fighting all the while to save my life, I had been alone. So, as I took action into my own hands to get myself home, it was no surprise that no one was going to help me – least of all the man who claimed to love me.

# 9

# Home

In the trauma unit, I was given a new member of staff for every issue I faced. I had a pain team that dealt with my medication, a nutritionist for my meals and a physiotherapist to help me with exercises. While Emile was rarely to be seen in the hospital, tagging along to my various appointments throughout the days was my key worker, a nurse who was there to support me and was my main point of contact with the clinical team.

'You ready for your next appointment, Vicky?' she smiled, appearing at my bedside, and I nodded. I knew she wouldn't leave my side now until a doctor had been and gone. I considered the various doctors' appointments a good way to break up the otherwise uneventful days but, as I saw the consultant approach us from the entrance of the ward, I couldn't help but feel nervous. I was due to find out the results from my x-ray and that would determine whether or not my spine needed to be operated on. *Please let it be stable*, I hoped as the doctor walked towards me. *I can't take much longer in here.*

'Hello Vicky,' the doctor greeted me, smiling warmly

as he took up his place beside my bed. 'How are you doing?'

'I'm good,' I replied, smiling back. 'Anxious to find out the results.'

'I bet,' he commented, flipping through the paperwork in front of him. 'Well, first of all, it's good news.'

'Really?' I asked, glancing at my key worker in relief.

'Yes, your spine is stable,' he answered. 'I don't think you'll be needing any more surgery.'

'That's great,' I replied, and it felt like a weight had been lifted. *One less thing to worry about.* I made myself a mental note to tell Emile later on. *Will he even care?*

'I've been having a look at your records,' the doctor continued, flipping through the notes in front of him. 'And I wondered if you'd considered speaking to a psychologist?' At first, I was taken aback.

'No, I hadn't,' I replied.

'You may benefit from it,' he said, looking up from his papers. 'You've been through quite an ordeal.' He smiled at me as I paused for a moment.

'I suppose it would be nice to talk to someone,' I decided, and the doctor nodded. I thought back to Emile's attitude towards me and all of the problems in our marriage I had kept hidden. *A psychologist might be someone I can confide in about it*, I realized.

'I'll make a note of it,' the doctor answered. 'And I'll have somebody come to see you.'

'Thanks,' I replied. It felt really good to know I'd finally be able to talk to someone about the real issues I was facing, but when the psychologist arrived on my ward a couple of days later, Emile had swung by to drop off some things from home.

'How are you, Vicky?' He smiled warmly, looking from me to Emile. 'You can either stay or go and grab a coffee while we chat,' he addressed Emile, who was sitting in the chair by my bed.

'I'll stay,' Emile shrugged, not moving from his spot.

'Are you happy with that?' the psychologist asked me. *What else can I say?* I wondered, knowing if I told Emile to leave it would be painfully obvious I wanted to discuss him. And I also knew he would use it against me if I ever complained about him not visiting. I could almost hear him say, *What about the time I came to see you and you told me you didn't want me there?*

'He can stay,' I answered, even though it meant this was now a waste of time. The psychologist started by asking how I was feeling about my accident, and I told him how frustrating it was to be away from April and Ben.

'It must be so hard,' he said, nodding reassuringly. 'And how's your marriage throughout all of this?' I could sense Emile looking at me in my peripheral vision.

'It's fine,' I lied, my heart sinking. Most of the time, Emile seemed to avoid the hospital at all costs, and yet the one time I wanted to be on my own, I couldn't get rid of him. After that day, I didn't bother to book another appointment. Once I thought about it a bit more, I realized that the psychologist was not really there to solve my marital issues. And I felt I was dealing with the trauma of the fall by shifting my focus back onto regaining my strength. Every day I felt more mobile than the last.

Initially, the physios gave me a large pulpit frame that I could lean my entire body on if I needed to. The first time I walked after the accident, it was with the aid of this frame. I wasn't allowed to put any weight on my right leg, as the force would go up to the right side of my healing pelvis. I could only let the toes of my right foot gently touch the floor for balance. Mustering all of my energy, I slowly shuffled four steps ahead. I felt euphoric. The small achievement gave me a glimmer of hope and, after that, I used the frame to move around my room. I worked hard to get stronger, to conquer the fresh challenges each new day brought, and soon after, I graduated to a Zimmer frame. When I no longer needed the Zimmer frame, I was given a pair of crutches. I smiled to myself, knowing this accomplishment also came with the privilege of walking myself to and from the bathroom at the end of the ward.

'I'm going for a shower,' were the first words that escaped my mouth upon being handed the crutches. The trip to the bathroom took longer than I had expected, and mentally it was a massive leap to go from the Zimmer frame to the crutches. I felt so shaky and unsupported, and it gave me a newfound respect for the patients I had worked with as a physio over the years. It may have only been a small step in the right direction, but walking myself out of the room in ICU to have a shower felt like I was finally regaining some independence.

Every time I made progress I was moved to a different room on the ward, and each time I was placed further away from the nurses' station to make way for patients with higher dependencies. *I'm getting closer to going home*, I realized, and every day I held on to the hope that I might get discharged.

'Right, Vicky,' a physio announced as she entered my room one day. 'I think you're ready for the stair assessment.'

Two physios stood with me at the bottom of a wide set of stairs in the hospital corridor. 'We're right behind you in case you fall,' one of them reassured me. 'But you've got to lift yourself up the steps.'

Taking hold of the banister, I pulled myself up the stairs before turning around and bringing myself back down. I had been given a brace to keep my back from bending, which made my steps slow and my movements rigid. Even so, I completed the stair test with ease, the drive to get back to my children burning as I went.

'We'll start looking at a discharge date for you,' the nurse told me, pleased with the progress I had made. 'Let's get you home.'

I beamed, not even able to believe myself that I had managed to shorten what should have been a three-month stay in hospital to just over two weeks.

'I can come home in a couple of days,' I enthused to

Emile on the phone later that day. 'Can you believe it?'

'Oh, no,' he quickly replied, his tone lowering. 'I've got too much on at work.'

'Oh,' I answered as my heart began to sink.

'I can't come and get you until several days after that.'

'I see,' I told him, but I felt deflated. *I've worked so hard*, I thought. *I've given my all to get to this point*. It felt like what Emile was really saying was that I was an inconvenience. My eyes welled up in frustration. *I want to see my children*, I cried to myself.

Three days later, which in hospital can feel like an eternity, Emile finally arrived to take me home. We barely spoke. I was still using the back brace that I had to wear at all times and I needed my crutches to walk, which made any awkward movements difficult. In silence, Emile helped me into the car, slamming the door while I clipped my seatbelt into place. As we set off, I racked my brains, trying to think of something, *anything* to say.

'I can't wait to see the kids,' I piped up, hoping to spark a conversation.

'Yeah,' Emile muttered, his eyes fixed on the road.

'Is April excited?' I asked, and he shrugged. Giving up, I sat back in my seat and fell into silence. *Why aren't you happy that I'm coming home?* I wondered, heartbroken by his indifference. Emile turned up the radio and I spent the rest of the car ride staring out of the window, thinking of holding my babies for the first time in weeks.

Once we pulled into the driveway, I couldn't wait to

get into the house, but my brace made everything a step-by-step process. I managed to open my car door and swing my legs to the side, but I needed Emile's help to lift me to my feet. *Does he wish I was still in hospital?* I thought, worried that I had made a mistake by coming home. We walked quietly to the front door and I waited as Emile fumbled with the keys.

As I walked into the house, April ran from the living room and immediately threw her arms around my legs.

'Mummy!' she exclaimed, squeezing me tightly. I found myself lost for words, wrapping my little girl up in a hug. I was overwhelmed by how happy I was to be back home with my babies. Hearing the commotion, Dad came into the hallway to greet me, Ben cradled in his arms. Without warning, I burst into tears.

'I can't believe how big he's got,' I spluttered, letting Dad carefully pass the baby over.

'Just take your time,' Dad tried to reassure me. 'You still need to rest.'

'I know,' I replied, but deep down I was already feeling inadequate. With me now home, Dad and Frances would be heading back to Scotland and I knew Emile was going to need help with the kids. *I can't add to his stress*, I thought. I hadn't taken into account how much harder it would be to recover at home than it was in hospital. There everything had been done for me, and suddenly I found myself frantically trying to keep up. When I had passed the stairs test in hospital, the banister had been strong and sturdy, starting right at the bottom of the stairs and leading all the way to the top. In our hallway, I looked at our stairs and was instantly intimidated. *The banister tapers off before the last step*, I realized, unsure of how I was going to manage. *I'll figure it out.* Taking one crutch with me, I slowly sat myself down on the bottom step and, putting my weight on my arms, I moved up each step on my bum. *When I get to the top, I'll use my crutch to stand up*, I told myself, but when I reached the top of the stairs, I couldn't get myself off the floor. I tried awkwardly to position my crutch but my brace made it impossible for my top half to bend. I was completely stranded.

'Emile,' I called out, and after a couple of seconds he appeared in the hallway below.

'What?' he asked, looking up at me.

'I'm stuck,' I admitted. My heart dropped as I watched him sigh before slowly trudging up the stairs to get me. Wordlessly, he crouched behind me and, placing his hands under my arms, heaved me off the step. 'Thanks,' I muttered, but Emile didn't reply. He went off to find April to give her a bath before bed, so I wandered into our bedroom. *I'll just stay here out of everybody's way*, I decided, feeling like a complete inconvenience. Emile seemed annoyed by how dependent I was on him. *I'm just another thing he has to deal with*, I worried to myself, hurt by how cranky he was being. *Perhaps if I was able to help him more, he'd calm down.* I remembered that Emile was still working full-time and wondered if that was the cause for his moods.

'I'll help out where I can with the baby,' I told Emile as we got ready for bed that night. 'I'll try to do my bit with the night feeds.' Barely two months old, Ben was still having regular bottles throughout the night.

'OK,' Emile agreed before rolling over. I struggled with my back brace, taking it off and placing it by the bed. Sleeping was the only time I was allowed to remove it, and even then I'd have to position myself flat on my back. I lay down carefully, and it felt like I had barely got to sleep when I heard Emile getting up to do the first feed.

'I'll pass Ben to you and I'll go make up his milk,' Emile said rather brusquely, rising to pick the baby up from his cot.

'OK,' I replied, trying to be as quick as I could. I lifted myself up from the bed and put the brace on. With my back fixed into one position, I was unable to sit down and hold Ben at the same time, so I stood in the bedroom, cradling him. As I waited for Emile to come back upstairs, I felt guilty at how annoyed he was getting.

'You may as well just go back to sleep,' he announced, taking Ben from me. 'There's no point in you being up.' The comment felt like a swift blow to the stomach.

'OK,' I mumbled, settling myself back into bed. *I'm not really needed or wanted here*, I thought, staring at the ceiling as I listened to Emile feed the baby. I went to sleep that night feeling completely worthless.

Yet I persevered, and after a couple of days things seemed to improve. It got to the point where Emile was almost being affectionate. My parents had gone back home and that seemed to make Emile more relaxed, laughing and engaging with me during the day and even sometimes giving me a cuddle on the sofa in the evenings. By now I was so used to his mood flying between hot and cold that I just enjoyed it while it lasted. Without Emile I was helpless, so I decided to take comfort in any emotional support he felt fit to offer. Nonetheless, he seemed happier to have me at home now and I started to relax, refocusing my mind on my recovery.

One weekend, we received a phone call out of the blue from the parachute centre to say the British Parachute Association were paying us a visit, and within an hour there was a knock at the door. I knew both my visitors – Jeff Montgomery had worked with me at Netheravon in the past and Tony was an instructor/examiner I'd met a few times.

'How are you doing, Vicky?' Jeff asked.

'I'm good, thanks. Come on in.' I showed them through to the living room, where Emile joined us.

'We just wanted to let you know in person that we've started an investigation into your incident,' they informed us, and I turned to look at Emile.

'Oh,' I replied, not knowing what to say. I had been so busy trying to get myself better that I'd barely given the accident a second thought.

'We want to get to the bottom of what happened,' Tony continued. 'I don't know if you've been told anything about it.'

'No, I haven't,' I admitted before pausing. 'Have you?' I added to Emile, and he shook his head.

'There were slinks missing in your parachute,' Tony told me.

I was stunned.

'What?' I asked, not knowing how to react. *That's impossible*. Up until this point I hadn't really considered how the incident had happened, and now it was a shock to hear it in detail.

'We're hypothesizing that it was only the pressure from the brake line, pushing against the other lines, that kept the parachute inflated enough for you to survive,' Tony informed us. 'Essentially, it's a surprise that you survived – you were a hair's breadth away from being killed.'

'I was lucky,' I muttered before crumbling. Emile hugged me as I broke down in tears, the news hitting me like a ton of bricks.

'It was a terrible accident,' Jeff continued. 'But we're going to find out what went wrong.'

'Thank you,' I told them. After we had waved them out of the door, I wondered how long it would be before I heard back. It wasn't until a few days later that my friend Alex called me from the parachute centre.

'Hi Vicky, I hope you're doing well,' she said warmly as soon as I answered the phone.

'I am, thanks,' I replied, grinning at the sound of a friendly voice. I had been doing a lot better since Emile's moods had picked up.

'I just wanted to give you a call because I've been talking with the chief instructor,' Alex continued. 'We're concerned about what's happened.'

'What do you mean?' I asked her, slightly distracted as April pestered me to play with her. 'You're concerned about the accident?'

'Well, we're not sure if it even was an accident,' she replied. 'We've looked over the parachute and the rig and something just doesn't add up.'

'What?' I asked. *That can't be right.*

'We want to report it to the police because we think it should be investigated properly,' Alex continued. 'I'm not going to do that without your permission though.'

'Oh, right,' I answered, unsure how to feel.

'What do you think?' she asked.

'I don't know,' I admitted, looking over at Emile who was buried in his phone. Any investigation would involve him too, and I knew he'd blame me if all hell broke loose. 'I'll need to talk to Emile first.' Hearing his name, he looked up.

'What's wrong?' he quizzed while I hung up the phone call.

'Alex wants to report the accident to the police,' I told him, trying to gauge his reaction. 'But I don't know what to do.'

Without a word, Emile got up from his seat and walked over to me, putting his arm affectionately round my shoulder.

'Yeah, you should, why not?' he replied.

'Well, what if it's nothing?' I asked him. 'I don't want to waste anyone's time.'

'If it's something that needs investigating then you

should let them investigate it,' Emile continued. 'Even if it's nothing, if it'll put everyone at the parachute centre's minds at rest then that's a good thing.'

'OK, I suppose you're right,' I replied, trusting Emile's opinion. As he wandered off into the kitchen, I picked up the phone again to punch in Alex's number.

'Hey,' she answered.

'If you don't think it was an accident then we think you should go to the police,' I told her. 'Let them investigate it.'

# 10

# The Investigation

'That's great to hear, I'm so glad you're on board,' Alex had said when I told her that the parachute centre could go to the police. 'I'll tell the chief instructor but I know it'll be such a relief for all of us.' *They must really have major concerns*, I thought upon hearing this. *But I'm sure there's nothing to worry about.* The idea that the fall might not have been an accident was starting to play on my mind, but even so, I couldn't see a feasible explanation for foul play. *How else could this have happened?* I wondered to myself, considering the fall to be nothing more than a freak accident. *There's no way the parachute was tampered with.* Even though it felt impossible that anything sinister could have happened to my kit, the notion that it could have terrified me. Nonetheless, it had been two weeks since Alex had reported the incident and I still hadn't been contacted by the police. *It must have been just an accident after all*, I assumed, guessing they had looked into it and found nothing worth investigating. I let the thought drift to the back of my mind. Besides, I had far too many concerns at home to deal with to even begin processing what had happened in the fall.

'Say no more,' one of my NCT group friends said as soon as I explained our situation. 'We'll plan April's birthday party for you.'

'Oh my gosh,' I replied, relief washing over me. 'You don't know how much this means to us.'

I'd joined the group when I was pregnant with April and the six of us shared a strong bond. Now the other women got to work, jumping at the chance to help us in our hour of need, and it felt so comforting to have them to rely on. I had assumed it would just be a small party at one of the mums' houses, not expecting them to take too much time out of their busy lives, but when we arrived I was blown away by the effort they had made. April was *Frozen* obsessed and, stuck in the house while recovering, I often found myself being forced to watch repeat showings with her throughout the day. I marvelled at the living room, which had been transformed into a Disney-themed party.

'Wow,' I exclaimed, admiring the incredible *Frozen* cake. 'You didn't have to do all of this.'

'Don't be silly,' one of the mums smiled. 'We're happy to help.'

They had arranged games and party bags, and in the garden was a bouncy castle where April and her friends spent all afternoon playing. Some of my other friends, Alex included, popped into the party to wish my girl a happy birthday and, while Emile took over care of Ben, I was free to laugh and socialize. After a couple of hours, I noticed Emile tucked away in the corner, rocking Ben gently, and I offered to give him a break but he wouldn't hear anything of it.

'Go and enjoy your day with April,' he insisted, looking for all the world like a doting dad. *What a switch he's made*, I thought to myself as I turned my attention back to April. I remembered the way Emile had behaved before Christmas, treating me like I was worthless, but now, four months later, it was like he was a completely different person all over again. I tried my best to enjoy my daughter's day as I struggled my way through the afternoon.

'That's great, April,' I spluttered, almost panting for breath as she showed me her presents.

'Are you OK, Vicky?' Alex turned to me.

'Yeah,' I replied, putting on a brave face. 'I'm just struggling to stay upright.' With the pressure of the spinal brace, an entire day spent on my feet with a crutch under each arm to hold me up was agony.

'Have you heard anything from the police?' Alex asked me as I took a break, carefully sitting myself down.

'No. I assumed you might have heard from them,' I told her, but Alex shook her head. I paused for a second. 'I guess it was just an accident then,' I added, but she didn't seem convinced.

'Maybe,' she replied. 'But even so, it doesn't make sense.'

Not knowing what else to say, I shrugged off her comment. I enjoyed the rest of the afternoon with my friends and that night, I returned home exhausted and in pain but with a full heart. I could barely lift Ben by myself so Emile carried him to bed, bathing April before joining me in the living room. He chuckled as he entered the room, seeing me lying flat on one of the sofas.

'You'd be lost without me,' he mused, sitting down on the other sofa.

'I would,' I replied, flicking through the TV channels. It had taken some time but things between the two of us appeared to be improving. *He's even laughing*, I noted, pleased by Emile's change of mood. *Things really are looking up.*

Two days after April's party, I was sitting at the kitchen table, feeding Ben his bottle, when I heard Emile run down the stairs in a panic.

'I'm late for work,' he announced, popping his head into the doorway. 'I've got to go but I'll see you later.'

'OK, I'll see you tonight,' I replied, listening to him open the front door.

'Bye!' he called out, slamming the door shut behind him.

'Looks like it's just the three of us today,' I cooed, chatting away to Ben from his baby chair. 'We've got the day to ourselves before Daddy returns.'

But Emile never came home. By the time he was due to arrive back from work, I was watching cartoons with April when there was a knock at the door.

'Come on,' I muttered to her as I heaved myself to my feet. 'Let's see who that could be.' I had no choice but to leave Ben on his play mat in the living room as I slowly made my way to the front door, a crutch tucked under each arm.

'Good evening, Mrs Cilliers,' one of the two men on my doorstep said as soon as I opened the door. 'I'm Detective Inspector Paul Franklin from Wiltshire Police.'

'Oh.' I paused for a second, taken by surprise. 'Hello.'

'May we come in?' he asked. I looked around at the chaotic house a day spent looking after two children while in a spinal brace had left me.

'Um, sure.' I led them into the living room and perched myself on the sofa. *What on earth could this be about?* I wondered, my mind racing with horrible possibilities. *God, I hope Emile is OK.* It suddenly dawned on me that I hadn't heard from my husband since the morning and, watching the officers sit down to face me, I started to panic. The pair of them were calm, cooing at the baby before turning their attention to me.

'We've come to visit you this evening, Victoria, because your husband has been arrested,' DI Paul Franklin told me, and I was stumped.

'What?' I asked, confused. 'What for?'

'He's been arrested on suspicion of your attempted murder.' Each word hit me like a train.

'He's what?' I asked, trying to process what they were telling me. 'Are you joking?'

'I know it must be a shock. He's currently being questioned at the station.'

*What the hell?* I thought, playing the officer's last sentence over and over again in my head. *Emile's been arrested for my attempted murder.* I didn't even suspect foul play, let alone that Emile would try to kill me. I heard the words but they just didn't make sense.

'I need to speak to my husband.' The words fell from my mouth without thinking. 'I need to speak to him.' But the other officer just shook his head.

'I'm sorry, Victoria, but you can't talk to your husband.' He glanced at DI Franklin then back to me. 'He's a suspect in an open investigation.'

'Why?' I asked, confused as to how this could have happened. 'Why do you suspect him?'

'Well, we have to talk to everyone that might have been involved, but that's all we can tell you right now.'

'When can I speak to him?' I quizzed. I didn't feel like any of this would make sense until I spoke to Emile. *He'll explain the misunderstanding*, I told myself. *We just need to sort this out.* He was my husband. I had married him and had children with him. I couldn't even begin to entertain the concept that he would be able to do something so inherently evil to me. I knew about his faults, but this was so far removed from them that it was unbelievable.

'I don't know how long it'll be before you can speak to him,' the officer admitted. Lost for words, I looked around the living room. April was tearing through her toy box without a care in the world while Ben giggled from his play mat. *How the hell am I going to look after these kids on my own?* I realized, the horror dawning on me. Before I could voice my concerns, the officer added, 'We do need you to come to the station to give a statement.'

I hesitated for a second, realizing I needed to do something about the kids.

'I'll have to ring my dad,' I told them in a daze. Not knowing what else to do, I reached for the phone and dialled his number.

'He's been arrested for *what*?' Dad blurted out as I explained the situation.

'I don't really know what's happening,' I admitted, suddenly feeling a lump in my throat. I looked around in a panic at April and Ben playing contently. 'But would you be able to come down here?'

'Of course, Victoria.' Dad's tone lowered to a more reassuring volume. 'We'll be there as soon as we can.' Driving down from Scotland meant it would be hours before Dad and Frances would arrive, so I called a friend, Jan, from the NCT group and quickly explained the situation. She agreed to come round to watch the kids while I went to the station.

'Mummy will be back in a bit,' I explained to April as I got ready to leave.

'OK,' April accepted, still busy with her toys. Giving her a quick kiss on the forehead and checking that Ben was fine, I left with the police officers. *Maybe I'll see*

*Emile at the station*, I hoped, but I quickly realized that was wishful thinking.

I was driven to Salisbury to make a statement on video.

'Can you tell me about the day of the jump, Vicky?' the officer behind the camera asked me. 'What happened once you jumped?' I took a deep breath.

'I knew something wasn't right straight away,' I replied, and suddenly my mind was thrown back to that day. I envisioned the tangled lines. 'There were a lot of twists and the canopy wasn't floating, it just wasn't flying properly, so I made the decision to cut away and deploy the reserve.'

'What happened once you opened the reserve parachute?' the officer continued. I shifted slightly, the pressure of the body brace feeling heavy on my chest.

'It was even more twisted,' I told him. 'The last thing I remember is trying to get some kind of control over it, trying to open it as much as I could, but then it all went black. I don't know if it was the effect of the g-force or the impact, but everything cut out.' Relaying the incident, all of the emotions from that day came flooding back and tears pricked at the corners of my eyes.

'What are your first memories from after the impact?'

'Um . . .' I hesitated, trying to remember. 'I know I opened my eyes and I saw the landing area, my friend was there and there were lots of people around, but that's just a brief snapshot. Another snapshot was inside the helicopter about to land, and then I don't remember anything until seeing Emile in A&E.' The officer nodded, taking down notes.

'Can you tell me about your marriage to Emile Cilliers?' he asked, and I struggled to answer initially. What do you say to a question like that?

'Is it a happy marriage?' he continued, and I paused. The question hit me like a punch to the stomach.

'Yes, it's fine,' I replied. *Every marriage has its problems*, I thought, too embarrassed to mention our issues with money and his infidelity. They asked for details about the days leading up to the jump, focusing on Emile's interaction with the parachute.

'It was rented kit,' I told him. 'He wouldn't have had much access to it on his own.'

'Was there any point before the jump that Emile was left alone with the parachute?' My mind raced, thinking back to the afternoon we had spent filling out forms at Netheravon. Suddenly, I remembered April had needed the toilet.

'She's a daddy's girl,' I explained. 'It made sense for Emile to take her.'

'He went into the toilet with the parachute on his back?' the police officer clarified, and I nodded. *This is damning*, I panicked, realizing just how serious the investigation was.

Before I left, they downloaded all the text messages from my phone so they could read through the messages Emile and I had sent to each other. I felt mortified and humiliated that intimate details of my marriage would be laid bare to these strangers.

'Here you go,' one officer said, handing the phone back to me. I was silent for a moment as the reality of my situation sank in.

'How do you expect me to cope without Emile?' I asked. 'You've just removed the person who looks after my kids.'

'There isn't a huge amount we can do,' the officer admitted. 'I know you've asked your dad to come down, so I assume you've got family support who can help you. We will contact social services and see if they can help.'

'What if I spoke to Emile in a safe environment?' I pleaded, needing to make sense of what was happening. 'Somewhere you can watch and listen.'

'No.' The officer shook his head.

'Please,' I begged. 'I just want to speak to him.'

'I know you do, Vicky,' he tried to reassure me. 'But he's under investigation.'

I fell silent, understanding the argument was futile. Knowing Dad was on his way should have been a comfort, but I just felt lost. The interview hadn't lasted long and, opening the front door after being dropped off at home, I could smell dinner being cooked in the kitchen.

'Hi Vicky,' Jan called over to me.

'Hi,' I replied. I shut the door behind me and rested my head against it. *What the fuck am I going to do now?* I wondered. I was completely incapacitated, unable to care for the children properly on my own, or even myself. I hobbled slowly to the kitchen. Lingering by the door, I saw April waiting patiently at the dinner table. *I won't even be able to get Ben upstairs at bedtime*, I realized. Leaning on one crutch, I fished my phone out of my pocket and opened a new message. Automatically, I began to type.

*What the hell is going on?* I wrote to Emile. *Why is this happening?* I waited for a few moments, staring at the blank screen hoping for a reply, but I never heard back from him. *How do I know if he's even got the message?* I asked myself, unsure if the police had taken his phone. Jan stayed with me overnight, helping me get both kids to bed.

I lay down that night and stared up at the ceiling, unable to sleep with how fast my thoughts were spinning. *How can everything change so suddenly?* I thought, devastated at what my life had become. Our marriage hadn't been perfect but I had thought things were improving. *He's clearly innocent*, I concluded, not knowing how the police could have got this so wrong. I couldn't, wouldn't, let myself contemplate the other option. I was in no fit state mentally to address that thought. I placed it in a box at the back of my mind. The apparent injustice of the situation I was in was all-consuming. I lay on my back in bed, removed the brace, and stabbed myself in the stomach with the nightly blood-thinning injection I had been prescribed. *Emile should be doing this.* I cried myself to sleep, longing for this nightmare to end.

\* \* \*

The next morning, Dad and Frances arrived at the house, relieving my friend of her childminding duties.

'Hi Victoria.' He greeted me with a sad smile as soon as I opened the door.

'Hi Dad,' I mumbled, letting him and Frances into the house. Once inside, Frances wrapped her arms around me, and I felt tears fill my eyes as I hugged her back.

'It's going to be OK,' she consoled, but hearing that made me cry harder. Ben's wails from the living room interrupted us.

'I'm not sure if it is going to be OK,' I replied, forcing myself to dry my eyes and see to my baby.

When the police returned to the house a few days later, my parents were still home to help with the children. This time, as I let the officers into the living room, I was ready with questions.

'When can I speak to Emile?' I asked as soon as they had sat down. 'Why do you suspect him?' It was unfathomable that Emile could have sabotaged my parachute, and I was angry that they were stopping my children from seeing their dad.

'You know you can't have any contact with Emile, and that goes for direct or indirect contact,' the officer replied. 'The bail conditions mean he's not allowed any contact with you either, and he's not allowed to enter Wiltshire.'

'Where is he then?' I questioned. It didn't make sense that they wouldn't even let Emile into the county.

'He's at his army accommodation,' the officer told me.

'We're actually here because we have some new information we think you need to know.'

'What is it?' I replied as Dad sat himself down beside me on the sofa.

'Well, we went to Emile's room at the barracks. We searched the place and we've spoken to him,' he continued. 'We've found pictures of his girlfriend in the room. There was nothing of you or the children in there.'

'What?' I asked. My cheeks blushed red and suddenly I was very aware that my dad was listening. *I had done such a good job of hiding our marital problems*, I cried internally. *And now all our dirty laundry is being aired.* I wanted the ground to swallow me up.

'He's been having an affair for a while – they had been planning on moving in together,' the officer kept talking. 'We've seen through text messages and from Emile himself that he had told her your marriage was over, that you had cheated on Emile and that Ben wasn't his son.'

Every piece of information they told me cut deeper and deeper.

'He's accrued lots of debts,' the officer added. *What?* I thought. I had known about the money issues but I had thought he was sorting things out. *He told me he'd cleared most of his debts – I gave him most of the money to do so. A final chance just before Ben was born*, I remembered. 'Essentially, he's been planning to set up a new life with his girlfriend.' I felt my blood boil.

'Nice,' I muttered, feeling the anger rise, not sure how to react. I was frozen to my spot on the couch, and I could tell the officers were waiting for me to respond. On the outside, I must have appeared emotionless, but inside I was raging. *First I have a stranger going through all of our personal things, and now my dad is having to hear about our problems.* There was no part of me that, even for a second, thought Emile was guilty of tampering with my parachute at this point. *But his actions and betrayal have caused all of this to be happening to me right now*, I seethed, furious with him. Breaking the silence, I ripped my wedding rings off my finger and flung them across the room.

'Victoria!' My dad tried to calm me down but now I couldn't even think straight. I sobbed hysterically, humiliated by what Emile had done. I cast my mind over what the officer had said. *Emile told that woman he wasn't Ben's dad*, I thought, and I just wanted to explode with anger. Instead, I howled uncontrollably, collapsing into my dad's arms. *What have I done to deserve this?* I looked up at the two officers, seeing a mixture of awkwardness and sympathy etched on their faces.

'Would you like to make a new statement?' one officer asked, and I paused. *How could Emile do this to me?* I raged, heartbroken by how much he'd used me. *He doesn't give a shit about me.* I reflected on all the issues I had left out of my original statement, so many things I hadn't said.

'Yes, I want to make another statement,' I replied, hot with anger. I went to the station and ranted for hours. All the problems I'd had with Emile over the years: the lies about money, the text messages from other women, the secretive holidays. It was like once I had started talking, I couldn't stop, scared that if I paused for breath I'd start to cry.

'The person I thought I knew does not appear to exist,' I choked out, and I felt as though our entire relationship had been a lie. 'It's a weird feeling.'

It was crushingly painful to remember the dizzy intensity of our first few years together. I had been the centre of his universe. We did everything together – we were a partnership with shared dreams for the future. Retiring together to South Africa once the children were established in life, to the plot of land his family owned overlooking the ocean. We had spent many occasions whiling away the hours discussing the house that we would build on the land.

'How do you feel?' the detective asked, offering me a tissue.

'Empty,' I admitted. I paused, wiping the tears from my eyes. 'Alone, angry. That this whole time I have had my little suspicions and niggles, and Emile made me feel really bad and blamed my past insecurities. My intuition was right – that makes me angry and upset. What I thought was a reasonable relationship and family, he's just torn apart.'

'The reserve parachute's error came from the failure of two crucial loops,' the detective said, reading through paperwork from the investigation. 'Could this have been an accident?' I thought it through, trying to find a feasible explanation, but I couldn't. I shook my head.

'I don't think it can be an accident,' I replied with a heavy heart. 'Slinks do not break, they really do not.'

'Has anything else odd happened recently?' the officer interviewing me asked. 'Anything strange besides the incident?'

Suddenly, my mind flashed back to the gas leak. *Emile reacted so oddly over it*, I thought, recalling how uptight and defensive he had been.

'Actually, yes,' I answered after a couple of seconds. 'Something strange happened about a week before the jump.'

I told the police everything they wanted to know about the gas leak. Through all of the questioning, though, I just wanted to speak to Emile. I had to know what was going on. *Why was he having an affair?* I wondered. *Why wasn't I good enough?* Emile had known about the infidelity in my first marriage and yet still saw fit to treat me badly and destroy our family unit.

'How long before I can speak to him?' I asked as I left the station.

'It'll be at least a couple of weeks,' an officer replied, and I nodded. *Just get through the next two weeks and then you can make sense of everything*, I told myself, but the sinking feeling in the pit of my stomach felt like a warning that any minute now, everything was going to fall apart.

# 11

# Picking Up the Pieces

In my fraught situation, my parents had taken over most of the childcare duties, but after the first couple of days, I could tell they were both struggling. Not just with the children – my dad was finding it hard to come to terms with the enormity of everything that was happening around us, and I knew I wasn't dealing with the investigation well. Every time a police officer stepped foot in the house, it felt like I was the one being accused. Social services had been contacted and were due to pay me a visit, but in the meantime I had a friend come over to stay with me.

'Go back home,' I told my dad, seeing the emotional toll it was taking on him. I didn't want this ordeal to affect him any further. 'I'm fine now.' I put on a brave face, giving him a tight hug before waving him and Frances off, but inside I felt lost. *You just have to focus on the kids*, I told myself, worried about how I would look after them without Emile.

I asked April's childminder if she knew anyone who could help, and she and two friends set up a rota for one of them to come in twice a day to help me out. I was beyond grateful, and before long I had got myself into a makeshift routine. In the mornings, one of the helpers would arrive at the house and come upstairs to carry Ben into the living room for me. They would help load the washing machine and clean any used dishes, taking laundry into the appropriate rooms. April would go to nursery for the day, but after that, Ben and I would be left to spend the day together. I could look after Ben from the sofa, having everything I needed to feed and change him within arm's length. In the evenings, April would return home along with another helper, who cooked dinner for the two of us while I fed Ben his bottle. Both kids would be bathed by the helper and Ben would be taken back upstairs for me.

It took a while, but I figured things out. The first time I was left on my own for the day, I laid Ben down on his play mat and headed into the kitchen to make lunch. *It'll have to be something easy*, I decided, peering into the fridge and noticing an unfinished salad. *Bingo*. I plated it up and poured myself a glass of water but, looking down at my lunch on the kitchen countertop, I realized I couldn't go anywhere. *Shit*, I thought. *I'm stuck*. I wasn't strong enough to carry the plate and so had no choice but to stand, with a crutch held firmly under one arm, and eat at the counter. *This isn't a feasible solution*, I thought, worrying about Ben in the other room. The next day at lunchtime, I looked around the kitchen, trying to figure out a way for me to take my food into the living room, when I spotted April's rucksack in the corner. *I could just carry my lunch in the bag*, it dawned on me, and for the next few weeks I lived off sandwiches, packing them up in a Tupperware container before storing it in the rucksack. I made myself a coffee in a travel mug and placed it in the bag to take with me to the living room. It felt like a small victory, working around the everyday tasks I was unable to do.

At night, however, I had no choice but to have Ben sleep next to me on the double bed.

'It's the only way I'll be able to feed him,' I told the helper, knowing I couldn't lift him out of his cot. Ben wasn't moving yet and I couldn't move anyway, so the pair of us lay side by side on the bed. *I'm making this work*, I thought, lying awake next to my sleeping baby. It wasn't ideal, but I had a sling in the bedroom in case there was an emergency and I needed to get Ben out of the house. I was finding my own way through it all.

In the evenings, I sometimes sat downstairs watching TV until I felt tired. My recovery was a long and lonely process. With both kids in bed, I was alone, left to fret and wonder when the chaos of the investigation was going to end. *I wouldn't mind a glass of wine*, I thought to myself one night. Using my crutches, I slowly made my way into the kitchen and pulled out a bottle of white wine from the fridge. I looked around the counter. *How am I going to bring it in the living room?* I reached for a glass from the cupboard and poured out some wine. Carefully, I tried to lift the glass, holding it in place as I started to make my way out of the room, but it was no use. No matter how slowly I moved, I couldn't help but spill the wine. *It's impossible*, I thought, searching around for anything to help me. Suddenly, I noticed April's sippy cup by the sink and smiled. I poured the wine into the sippy cup and carried it through to the living room. Switching between the channels, I sipped on the wine with a small sense of accomplishment. *We're going to get through it*, I thought. *I can figure this out.*

Being stuck at home had one advantage, in that I didn't have to face the world when news got out about Emile's arrest, though I did have a reporter ringing my doorbell about a week after it happened. I refused to talk to them but nevertheless a story appeared in the *Mail* quoting unnamed sources, illustrated with a photograph of me at my door that I had not realised was being taken. While I was in hospital I'd set up a Facebook page just for close friends and family, so I could update them on my progress, and I had added a sad and bewildered statement on Emile's arrest. A few sentences from that were quoted in the paper. It was the first warning sign of what would become an overwhelming media scrutiny that would leave me feeling horribly exposed and, in some cases, betrayed by people I trusted. Thankfully I had no idea then what was in store for me.

Every day, I forced myself to exercise, to start rebuilding my body. A colleague helped me to set up a rehabilitation programme and I was loaned a stationary bike to cycle on. My physio expertise kicked in. *This is what I do best*, I thought as, day in, day out, I worked hard to re-educate my muscles. I practised my range of movement, teaching myself to walk properly again while building my fitness. In the safety of my own home, my only witness was Ben, peering up at me with wide eyes as I exercised. The more I trained, the more my daily life seemed to become more bearable, and each achievement felt like a huge relief.

Physically, I was becoming stronger, but the chaos surrounding my life seemed to continue to grow. All I wanted was answers, but each time I spoke to the police, the more confused I was left about what was going on.

'Can I see Emile now?' I asked as I reached the end of the two-week period.

'It's complicated,' my liaison officer replied. 'We still need to do more work.'

'Well, how long is it going to be then?' I asked him. I hoped that if I could talk face to face with Emile about everything – the affair, the accusation that he had tried to kill me – I would be able to see the truth in his eyes, hear it in his voice. 'I need to speak to Emile.'

'It'll be at least another month,' the officer told me. I had no choice but to nod. *I just have to get through the month*, I told myself, but when the month came to an end, the police simply extended the period further.

As my recovery continued, I started to become more mobile. After three months I was able to carry Ben up the stairs to bed. The first time I did it, with Ben in a baby carrier strapped to my body, I was petrified that I might slip. But my movements were steady and, lowering him into his crib, I smiled down at my precious baby, proud of how far I had come. Being able to pick Ben up and then being able to leave the house without assistance were big steps. I tried to focus on getting better but, with Emile banned from contacting me, it felt like my life had been put on hold.

Social services had visits with the children every ten days. I also had to attend monthly meetings where, along with the social worker, there would be a healthcare worker from my GP's surgery and a representative from April's nursery. Thankfully I had an army welfare worker present too, who was at least on my side. I felt as if social services treated me like a child they were trying to placate. They were pleasant enough, but I couldn't help wondering if the police were using them as their eyes and ears in my house. I was obligated to contact them if we were sleeping anywhere else but at home, and it was frustrating to have restrictions placed on us. I would often be invited to spend time with friends and stay over at their houses so we could have a drink together, but I felt that that was no one else's business.

'If you try to leave the country,' a social worker informed me, 'you'll be apprehended at the airport and the children will be removed from you.' *Why am I the one being treated like a criminal?* I thought to myself. *They're giving me no freedom to breathe.*

April was too young to question why Daddy wasn't

staying with us any more, and she and Ben were still seeing Emile in sporadic visits. His ban from entering Wiltshire was overturned and Carly would arrive to pick the kids up to see him. *How strange*, I mused to myself as I watched Carly's car pull out of the drive. *I'm the only person not allowed to see him.*

By now, the police were coming to the house on a regular basis, so it was no surprise when I answered the phone one morning to my liaison officer.

'Hi Vicky,' he chirped down the phone. 'Just to let you know we're coming round today to have a chat.'

'Right,' I replied, looking over at the clock on the wall. It had just gone eight in the morning. 'I'll see you soon.'

Once the phone call clicked off I did my best to make the place look straight, and before I knew it there was a knock at the door. *I hope this doesn't take too long*, I thought as I made my way into the hall. *I've got a dentist appointment.* I opened the front door, expecting to see one or two officers standing in front of me, but when I looked up, I gasped. Two police vans stood parked on the front with what felt like an entire army of officers.

'What's going on?' I asked, stunned by the number of people waiting to come in.

'We're here with a warrant to search your property,' one of the officers said.

'Oh,' I replied. *That's bloody great.* Lifting Ben from his play mat with a timid April hiding by my side, I watched the officers march inside and begin the search.

'Mummy,' April asked, tugging on my jumper. 'Why are all of these people in our house?' I looked down at my little girl, lost for words.

'They're just doing work,' I replied after a moment, gently brushing the hair from her face. *What do I do?* I wondered, looking at the mess they were creating around us. *Fuck it*, I decided. *I'm going to the dentist.* Strapping both kids into their car seats, I drove away from the house, knowing I couldn't do anything to stop what was happening at home.

I took my time running errands and dropped April off at nursery on the way back, but when I returned, the police were still wading through my things. The carpets had been ripped up and everything from the garage pulled out. *Gosh*, I thought in horror. *They're destroying it.* It was as if the house was being tipped upside down and shaken until there was nothing left. I could hear a lot of noise coming from the kitchen and so, placing Ben back onto his mat in the living room, I headed in to see what was happening. I watched a gas specialist remove the valve from the metal pipe by the cooker, inspecting the dried blood around the lever. When I moved back into the living room, I spotted a policewoman bent down talking to Ben. She wasn't touching him or trying to pick him up, but all of a sudden I felt a surge of irrational rage.

'Don't talk to my son,' I snapped, rushing to scoop up my baby. 'Don't go near him.'

I wanted to scream with anger and frustration. I knew

she hadn't done anything wrong but I couldn't help it. Seeing my house be torn apart was traumatizing, and seeing a stranger engaging with my little boy felt disrespectful. I took Ben upstairs and waited for the nightmare to be over. When evening rolled around, everyone finally left. Although they had largely put the house back as they found it, I could see that things weren't in quite the right place. I walked around, hastily tidying up, binning my bedsheets and anything else they'd touched. *I have no control over my life*, I realized in dismay. The thought of complete strangers rifling through all of my personal items made me feel violated.

Every time I had contact with the police or social services, the anxiety I felt would trigger flashbacks in the middle of the night. Instead of sleeping I'd be on the plane again, hiding my tears, wishing I wasn't there. Or I'd be in free fall, spinning violently as I fought for my life. Even when I slept I'd sometimes – not often – have nightmares where my fall would end with me hitting the ground. It got to the point where I couldn't watch any television programme about the emergency services as the sound of sirens would trigger the memories. Once, I couldn't sleep for two whole nights as I replayed the fall over and over again.

This was a particularly hard and heartbreaking time that seemed never-ending. All my hopes and dreams, which had already been running thin prior to the parachute jump, were now imploding in front of me. I had no control over any aspect of my life except what was going on in my head. I had to have hope. Hope was the only thing that got me through this. Hope that the man I loved and married hadn't tried to kill me, hope that one day I wouldn't have to explain to the children what their father did. He had shown himself to be a cold and uncaring liar, but a murderer? I could not and would not let that thought take hold.

Prior to his arrest, Emile and I had discussed the possibility of taking a holiday to South Africa at Christmas time, but also I wanted the freedom to take the children away if I wanted. I had applied for a passport for April soon after she was born and so, not giving it a second thought, I applied for Ben's passport. *It all might be sorted by December*, I hoped. *It surely can't take that long*. But a few days later, I had a visit from one of the detectives.

'We know you've applied for a passport for Ben,' he told me. 'You do know you cannot leave the country.'

'Well, I haven't done anything wrong,' I argued back. 'Why am I the one who's getting punished?'

I can only assume they thought I might run off with Emile – who, ironically, *was* allowed to go abroad. I had heard from friends that he was completing sporting events around Europe and making trips to South Africa to see his family. The man suspected of killing me had more freedom than I did!

By the time of our wedding anniversary, it had been four months since I had last seen Emile, and that weekend an officer was sent to drop another bombshell.

'Emile has now also been arrested for your attempted murder with the gas leak,' he told me. 'And because the children were in the house at the time, he is no longer allowed any access to them.'

'God,' I replied. I could feel myself freezing up, searching helplessly for the words to say.

'April and Ben are being placed on the children's protection register,' he continued. 'Because they are at risk from Emile.'

I felt completely isolated. I was angry at Emile for putting me in this situation, and I also felt angry at the police for not being honest with me.

'I'm not speaking to Emile any time soon, am I?' I asked, knowing before the officer replied that there was no definitive end to this.

'No,' the police officer shook his head. 'You're not.'

With no chance to try to get the truth from my husband, and with the police not giving me any evidence to look through, I was left not knowing what to think. *Is he guilty?* I wondered yet again, trying to imagine a world where Emile would want to kill me. When I thought of Emile, it was as though I was thinking of two different people. There was the original Emile I had fallen in love with, who was an intensely caring, loving, dynamic family man – and then there was the other Emile. He was cold and detached, and I didn't recognize the person I was married to in the last few months before the fall. *Are either of them capable of killing me?* It just didn't seem possible.

A few months after the initial arrest, prior to the additional gas leak charge, the bail conditions were relaxed to allow Emile into Wiltshire.

When it could be arranged, I brought the children to a contact centre as Emile was now allowed to spend time with them. Watching them be taken off into another room by a supervisor was painful, but the wait on the other side of the door was worse. Sometimes, I'd sit listening to April laugh at something Emile had said to her, and I'd spend the car ride home in tears. Meanwhile, the children would sit in the back, giggly and chatty from the visit, and I would have no choice but to put on a brave face in front of them.

Even harder to deal with were the continuous questions coming from April that I just didn't have the answers to.

'Where's Daddy?' she asked me constantly. 'Why can't I speak to him?'

'He's at work, sweetheart,' I told her, not knowing what else to say. He was not allowed contact with them outside the contact centre.

'Well, can't you FaceTime him?' she replied, pointing at my phone. She was used to speaking over video chat with my parents on a weekly basis, and the fact that she couldn't access Emile as easily was confusing for her. Sometimes she got angry. 'Just call him up!' she screamed, throwing the phone at me in frustration. It broke my heart to see her so unsettled.

'I've told you, April, Daddy's at work,' I repeated,

trying to calm her down. A lot of her anger and upset was directed towards me, and I didn't know what to tell her because I had no idea what was happening. *I can't promise her one thing*, I thought, *and then something else happens.*

As the months passed, I was still none the wiser as to whether Emile was going to be formally charged. Every time I reached the deadline set by the police, the point at which they had said I could talk to him, they raised the bar, so it felt as though I was in a race that I was never going to win.

I had been played like a puppet by Emile and now the police made me feel powerless too. I felt like no one really cared about how it was affecting me. To the world, I had to put on a front and pretend that everything was all right, but when I returned to the safety of my home, I was a wreck. Not wanting to get up in the morning or go out of the house, I just didn't want to function. I survived minute by minute purely for the sake of the children. *There's no other reason to exist any more*, I thought. *My life isn't my own.* I was mentally and emotionally exhausted.

Even though I still couldn't really believe Emile was a killer, it was at this point that fear started creeping in. I started having nightmares where Emile was standing over me as I slept. I'd wake up with a jerk, my heart pounding, expecting to see him there in the dark.

Incrementally, my life seemed to be on a downward

spiral. *Am I going mad?* I sometimes wondered, often finding myself talking to Emile in my head. When things were going wrong – if the kids were both ill and I'd been up all night, or if I didn't know how to resolve things – I'd ask Emile for help, trying to predict what he would say in these situations. It didn't feel fair that I had been left to make all of the big decisions on my own. April was still regularly asking when she could see her daddy, which was heartbreaking. Not knowing what else to do than continue to say that he was away with work, I went to see a psychiatrist.

'This is just a normal reaction to an abnormal situation,' was all she could come up with. *Great*, I thought. *That doesn't really help me.*

I persevered for April and Ben, taking each day as it came, and when my maternity leave ended in late December 2015, I returned to work. It was incredibly intimidating. This being the military, most of the people I knew had moved on and I spent many sleepless nights worrying that I'd be stared at and whispered about, and that I'd struggle physically with being at work. In the end, everyone treated me normally, and I was given a bespoke chair and desk that helped prevent any hip or back pain.

After work, I'd come home to make dinner, picking up April and Ben from the childminders on the way, and once I had them settled in bed for the night, I'd spend the evenings studying. I had earned a place on a Sports Physiotherapy Masters programme before the fall, but had not been able to study while I was recovering from my injuries. Now I really applied myself and graduated in August 2016 with a merit. *Not bad*, I thought with a smile when I learned the result. I was determined to secure a future for my babies. Without Emile here, I felt a newfound pressure to succeed for the sake of the kids, and without someone with me to share the burden, it seemed that my worries doubled. The friends from my NCT group were always on the end of the phone when it simply all got too much – to offer advice, wine or just listen. But as supportive as they were, I did feel like the odd one out for a while as the only lone parent.

When Ben was eighteen months old and just learning to walk, I first felt the full weight of being a single parent. Discovering strength in his arms, one morning Ben pulled himself up on a radiator in the living room. With my back turned for just a few seconds, he gripped onto the red-hot heater and started to scream.

'Oh my god!' I gasped, running to pick him up. Examining his sore hand, I rushed him to the kitchen sink and held his palm under the cold tap. Every sob Ben let out felt like a punch in the stomach as I tried to soothe the pain, but when I looked down at his hand, I could see the skin on his palm was bubbling into blisters.

'I think we're going to have to get you to a doctor,' I sighed, wrapping my baby in a tight hug. I gathered up my things, taking April to nursery on our way to the hospital. *Thank god it's not busy*, I thought as I carried

Ben into A&E. *Hopefully we won't be waiting long.* Ben was seen almost immediately, with a nurse taking us into a cubicle to dress his wounds.

'Oh dear,' she cooed to him as I wiped the tears from his eyes. 'We'll fix you right up.'

'Thanks,' I added as she fastened the bandage around his hand. The nurse smiled but, moving to the computer in the corner of the cubicle, her face fell.

'I'll be back in a minute,' she told me, abruptly leaving the room. *Where is she going?* I wondered, bouncing Ben on my knee. I could see the nurse talking on the phone through the window of another room. She was gone for a while and when she came back, her manner had changed.

'I've just spoken with social services,' she announced as I sat in shock. 'We need to get a paediatric consultant to authorize you leaving the hospital with Ben.'

'What?' I asked, confused. 'Why?'

'Ben is flagged on the system as being on the protection register,' she explained. 'It means we have to get social services involved if we think they're at risk.'

'Oh,' I muttered, trying to process what she was saying. Slowly, the horror dawned on me. *She thinks I'm trying to hurt my child*, I realized, wanting the ground to swallow me up. The nurse directed me to the children's ward where I waited for hours with Ben. *I feel like the scum of the earth*, I thought, sure that everyone who looked over at us was judging me. When the consultant was finally free, I was shown to his office, where Ben was checked over for any signs of abuse.

'OK,' the doctor eventually told me. 'You need to go back to children's social services for authorization and then you can go home.'

'Right,' I replied, carrying Ben back out of the ward. I had to get one of the nurses to call for me as there was no mobile reception. It was humiliating and I had to fight back the tears. When I finally got home, I felt defeated. On autopilot, I made dinner before tucking both kids in, but once alone on the sofa, the crashing lows from the day's events surfaced. *Oh, get a grip*, I told myself, wiping the tears from my eyes. *Stop focusing on the negative stuff.* I tried to consider the positives: I had two healthy children, a job and a roof over my head. *There are many people worse off*, I tried to tell myself, but it didn't change my reality. Stuck in a constant rollercoaster of emotions, I couldn't see the wood for the trees. I felt completely trapped by what Emile had done, and the truth of it was that I just didn't want to exist any more. Life simply wasn't worth living. But at the same time, I knew there was no way out because of the children. *I have to function for them*, I reminded myself. *They deserve a happy upbringing and that means I have to keep going.*

Over the months of the police investigation, plenty of people would comment on how well I was coping. 'I don't know how you do it,' they'd marvel. *I've got no fucking choice*, I wanted to reply. *I have to.* Sometimes it was simply existing from one hour to the next, getting through one bath-time or dinner to prepare. There was no respite from the sadness and stress, and it was slowly breaking me.

When I walked into April's room one morning after three consecutive days and nights of relentless vomiting from a bug and saw that she barely had the energy to open her eyes, I felt like the worst mother in the world. *What do I do?* I panicked, knowing that she needed to see a doctor. I watched with concern as she threw up until there was nothing left in her stomach, and after that she retched uncontrollably. My poor baby was so sick that she couldn't even walk and, carrying Ben with April in his pushchair, I took them both to the doctors.

'She'll recover soon,' the doctor tried to reassure me. 'You need to try to get small sugars and fluids into her.' *How am I supposed to do that?* I thought to myself, well aware that April wasn't keeping anything down.

*I don't want to take her to A&E*, I panicked once we returned home. *I don't want to go through that again.* Seeing how sick my daughter was, I felt torn. Ultimately, I wanted to do the best by her, but the thought of facing another day of questioning at the hospital seemed almost too much to bear. *I have no choice*, I told myself. *She needs a doctor.* One of my NCT friends, Jane, came to pick up Ben before I rushed April to A&E.

'I'll look after him for as long as it takes,' she reassured me. This time, I called social services, but I was a nervous wreck. *What if something serious happens one day and there's no one to help?* I stressed. *What if something happens to me?*

I knew I had been lucky to have someone nearby but the next time there was an emergency, I was completely on my own. In an attempt at continuing with normal life, I had taken both kids for a day out at Moors Valley Country Park when the worst happened – Ben broke his arm while playing. Between his wails, I phoned for an ambulance, but when the paramedics arrived I realized I was stuck.

'We'll take him to Dorchester Hospital,' they told me, which presented an obvious problem. *How am I going to get home?* With my car parked up at Moors Valley and with April to look after, I found myself in an impossible situation. *Ben is too young to ride alone in the ambulance*, I thought, ruling out that option. *And he'd be too upset if I even tried to leave him with the paramedics*. With my little boy hysterically crying, I had to make a decision.

'No,' I decided. 'I'll drive him myself.' Strapping Ben into his seat and buckling April's belt, I drove the three of us to the hospital, and she cried the whole way there. By the time we arrived it was getting late, and I was juggling Ben with his broken arm and an increasingly restless April. A&E was busy and it was hours before we were finally seen. With both kids now in full meltdown mode, I almost wanted to howl myself. *Oh my god*, I thought, the screams piercing my ears. *Please just let us go home*. Finally Ben's arm was put in plaster and we were allowed to leave. Parking up the car in the drive, I got both children into bed before I crumpled onto the landing floor and cried.

During this period Emile's absence was ever apparent, especially for April, who had always been a daddy's girl. When I took the children to a park one afternoon, out of nowhere my daughter burst into tears.

'I want my daddy here too,' she cried, gazing around at all of the other families soaking up the sun.

'I know you do,' I replied. I tried to scoop her up in my arms but she wriggled free.

'Why won't you let Daddy come with us?' she sobbed, and it broke my heart. I knew why she was angry – she couldn't possibly understand why Emile wasn't here – but I didn't have the answers she craved.

It felt like the police investigation was never going to end, and I didn't know how much more I could take.

It was almost two years after the fall when the CPS finally made a decision, in January 2017. That morning, I arrived at work knowing Emile had a bail hearing that day. *God,* I stressed to myself, not knowing what was going to happen, *I hope this ends soon.* I spent the day with anxious knots gripping my stomach, but the busy atmosphere helped to distract me.

'The boss wants to see you, Vicky,' one of my colleagues told me in the afternoon.

'Oh, OK,' I replied, getting up to head towards his office, but when I opened the door, my boss wasn't alone. Beside him stood two police officers – my heart sank.

'Hi Vicky,' one of the officers smiled. 'Mind if we have a quick chat?'

'Sure,' I replied, stepping into the room. I sat myself down on a chair, waiting for whatever bad news they were going to impart this time.

'A decision has been made,' the officer told me, and I held my breath.

'Oh,' I muttered. Just by his tone of voice, I knew what was coming next.

'Emile is being formally charged with your attempted murder on two counts, and reckless endangerment of the children's lives.'

I felt the world crash around me. Although I had had moments when I was fearful that Emile was guilty, they were just moments. I hadn't really believed it, telling myself that this was a mistake and that at some point the police would realize it. To think otherwise was simply too painful. But now reality started to hit. Clearly there was evidence that was compelling enough to charge him.

*Why me?* I thought. *What have I done to deserve this?* I felt the tears welling up in the corners of my eyes and I couldn't help but cry. For a few seconds, I didn't say anything, too upset to speak.

'Can I talk to him now?' I finally asked, knowing by now that the question was futile.

'No, Vicky,' he replied, and his face was full of pity. 'You're going to be called as a witness in Emile's trial.'

*Emile's trial*, I repeated to myself. *He's going to stand trial.* I had been so focused on wanting this nightmare to end, I hadn't realized that it was only just beginning.

# 12

# The Trial

*What if my fall was deliberate?*

Knowing that this question would be coming up in court sent my brain into overdrive, replaying the incident over and over again, running through all the possible options on an endless loop. I knew there were a few scenarios the police had considered. Emile, of course, could have been the culprit, or perhaps someone else at the parachute centre. If it was someone else then they couldn't have been targeting me, as no one else could have known I was about to rent the kit. Detectives had asked if I had done it to myself, and that notion was almost laughable although I understood that they had to consider this, not knowing me. It could have been equipment failure but that seemed extremely unlikely. I knew how strict the checks at the parachute centre were. *Those are the alternative options*, I reminded myself. *And none of them seem as likely as Emile.* That possibility had been locked away in my mind but now I felt as if I was being forced to put a key in the lock.

At home with the kids, I was a sitting duck. Emile was

not in prison – he was out on bail, free to travel wherever he pleased in the run-up to his court case. *If he wants to kill me, there's nothing stopping him,* I worried. *He knows where to find me.* My stress and fear mounted. But with little information from the police, I had no choice but to carry on with daily life in the hope that nothing bad would happen. At least my job gave me something to focus on, and helping other people was a welcome change from feeling helpless myself. By now I was a clinical specialist, having been promoted in July 2018 and given more managerial responsibility. I pushed myself at work, and at home I tried to keep the children happy, occupied and well rounded. Essentially I was a robot and I struggled in the evening, when the children were asleep and – alone with my thoughts – I went over and over Emile's treatment of me and felt as if I had totally failed in life.

After time had dragged on for what felt like an eternity, now it was hurtling forward and I couldn't stop it. Once I was told I would stand as a witness, I wished for things to slow down again.

'He must be guilty, Vicky,' friends tried to say, but that just made me feel worse.

'I don't know what to think,' I admitted. I hated being told what to believe and felt again like I was being backed into a corner.

'But he had an affair and pretended Ben wasn't his,' another friend piped up. 'And he's racked up so much debt.'

'I know he did all of those things,' I snapped back,

upset by the comments. 'I don't need constant remind-ing.' *But being a terrible husband doesn't make you a murderer,* I added to myself, and that would remain my stance in the lead-up to the trial.

Finally, two and a half years after the fall, in October 2017 the trial began. I knew I wouldn't be allowed in the courtroom until after I had stood as a witness. That almost felt like a relief, to avoid that pressure. Still, my mind rattled with the possible scenarios of what was to come. I spent the day anxiously checking the news and looking through my phone. Eventually an article popped up. Without thinking, on autopilot, I opened it.

> The court heard today that on April 5, 2015, Victoria Cilliers was involved in a near fatal parachuting fail in Netheravon, Wiltshire. Those at the scene immediately realized that some-thing was seriously wrong with her parachute. Two vital pieces of equipment, slinks which connect the harness to the para-chute, were missing and their absence meant the reserve parachute would send her spiralling to the ground.

None of what I read was new to me, but seeing it all laid out – written by a journalist for a news article – brought it home. It was incredibly upsetting to read.

> Emile Cilliers had started an affair with Stefanie Goller after meeting her on Tinder and in WhatsApp messages, Cilliers lied that Victoria had given birth to a child that was not his as a result

of an affair. The jury also heard that Cilliers was involved in a sexual relationship with his ex-wife, Carly Cilliers.

I paused. Hearing more detail about Emile's affair with Stefanie left me sick to my stomach, but learning about Carly completely floored me. I sank to my knees in the kitchen, reading and re-reading the article. We had never been friends as such but we had, I thought, a reasonable relationship. She had been on hand to help when I needed childcare, even looking after Ben when I had to attend medical appointments. The pair of them together, behind my back, whilst I was heavily pregnant and after Ben was born . . . I couldn't bear to think about the added betrayal.

Instead, I skimmed through the rest before landing on a paragraph that stood out.

In 2015, Cilliers had debts of around £22,000 and allegedly believed he would receive £120,000 from an insurance policy in the event of his wife's death.

I stopped for a moment. The new information felt like almost too much to take in. *Could Emile be capable of hurting me?* I wondered. *If he thought he stood to inherit money?* The idea made me feel even worse.

Over the next few days, I pored over the news updates, reading how the chief instructor at the parachute centre had been called in to offer his expertise.

'Vicky landed in an exceptionally soft field, it had just

been ploughed,' he had told the court. 'That, combined with her light weight and the fact that the jump was lower than usual, contributed to her survival.'

'Could the slinks have broken mid-fall?' Michael Bowes, the prosecuting barrister, asked.

'It's extremely unlikely,' he answered. 'The slinks are such a strong piece of equipment. Had the shock been so much to break two slinks I would expect to have seen some damage to other pieces of equipment, but I didn't. Instead I found, and what I thought was most unusual, was that there was not only no damage but actually there was no visible sign that either of the lines had been under load. I began to wonder if the slinks had ever been there at all.'

'Is there any way this could have happened innocently?' Mr Bowes continued.

'The only innocent theory I have for the missing slinks from the reserve is if they had been cut off by one of the first-aiders or medics at the scene, but I checked this and I found that no one had cut anything apart from her goggles strap,' he replied. With foul play considered likely by the chief instructor, Emile's trip to the toilet with April – with the parachute rig swung over his shoulder – was being discussed at great length.

'It's heavy and bulky,' the prosecution lawyer told the court. 'There was absolutely no reason to take it in there at all. The weather was so poor that afternoon that Victoria couldn't jump – the cloud base was too low – but now, of course, that was a dilemma because what was he going to do with the rig, having tampered with it? He couldn't put it back in the store. Instead he arranged to keep it overnight in his wife's locker against normal procedures at the base, where its parachutes were always returned to the kit room overnight.' Hearing the reports, my mind raced back to the day in question. *It was against normal procedure*, I noted. *But I was an instructor.*

The lawyer had also analysed Emile's behaviour that day.

'Mr Cilliers was acting out of character, keeping track on the weather forecast that afternoon. He was really, really keen that she jumped, a woman who by this point he couldn't care less for any more, the woman he wanted to abandon. Suddenly he is so concerned that she has a good time parachuting.'

Knowing all of this had been talked about in court made me feel sick and over the next few days it triggered more flashbacks of the fall. Various people who had witnessed the incident had told police that they had heard screams, seeing me thrash helplessly as I plummeted through the sky. The first ones on the scene had been so sure I would be found dead that they had brought a body bag. Instead they had found me alive, drifting in and out of consciousness.

'It's a miracle she survived,' the prosecution lawyer concluded.

Online, the headlines were damning. *Army sergeant 'tried to murder wife so he could run off with Tinder lover,'* they read. '*Love-rat' Cilliers accused of tampering*

*with wife's parachute 'went on advanced packing course'.*
Reading the details of our lives plastered across the internet was humiliating. *I don't want anything to jeopardize
us*, Emile's texts to his girlfriend read, sprawled out on
the page of a newspaper. *You have no idea how much
you mean to me.* It was devastating.

Between the articles and news bulletins, my dad was
checking in on me often.

'Frances and I are here whenever you need us,' he
reminded me over the phone. 'Don't forget that.' When
it was nearing the time for my court appearance, they
packed up the car and drove down to Wiltshire to be
with me.

'Thanks for coming down,' I told him as he wrapped
me in a hug. 'I know it's hard for you.'

'Where else would I be?' Dad smiled. I tried to make
the evening as normal as possible, with the five of us
sitting down to a family dinner, but the night before my
first day in court I lay awake for hours, wondering what
the day ahead would bring. Restless, I looked through
the news articles on my phone. Every detail was being
dragged through the trial, even text messages Emile and
I had sent to each other. *Are you trying to kill me?* The
text I had typed after the gas incident rang in my ears,
paraded by the prosecution through the court. *Oh god*,
I panicked. *Am I really ready for this?* The sudden real-
ization that I would finally be face to face with Emile
dawned on me, and it was gut-wrenching. *Will he even
look the same?*

The next morning, Dad and Frances went to Winchester together to watch the trial from the public gallery. At my request, they wouldn't be travelling with me. I made my way to the courthouse with Nikki, an army welfare support officer, dropping April and Ben with a childminder along the way. The childminder would take April to and from school.

'Have a brilliant day,' I told April, planting a kiss on top of her head. *The more I can protect the kids from this, the better*, I told myself, relieved to see that, at least for now, they seemed unaffected by it all. I made sure that April never saw any news bulletins on the TV, as did the childminder. Ben was still too young to pick up on what was happening.

With the children looked after, we drove to Winchester Crown Court, but as we approached the courthouse, I caught a glance over the road of a group of reporters waiting on the steps. *Oh god*, I thought. *I can't cope with that*. Desperate to avoid the unwanted attention, I made a point to park round the back, trying to slip through unnoticed. We were guided through the building by a member of court staff until we came to a table and chairs. There, I waited with Nikki, and at first her dry sense of humour got me through most of my nerves. But as the time for my appearance drew closer, I fell silent, apprehension lying thick between us. *What is there to say?* I thought, at a loss for words when, without warning, I was called into the courtroom.

I followed a member of staff, taking a deep breath

before walking through the entrance. I had half expected to see Emile nearby, to be able to make eye contact. I hoped that looking into his eyes might give me a clue as to his guilt. Would I see the loving husband I'd lived with for the first few years of our relationship, or the hard and cold man he became? But the room was massive and he had been placed as far away as possible. I made my way to the stand, peering over at the figure in the distance. Sitting behind glass and staring at the floor was my husband. From where I stood, I could barely make him out. From that point I tried not to look at him. *Just answer the questions and get out*, I told myself.

My attention was grabbed by a lawyer approaching the stand and, before I knew it, I was being asked about the trip to the hangar toilet Emile had taken the day before my fall.

'In your first interview you had told police Emile was gone for a couple of minutes,' he said, and it quickly felt like I was the one on trial. 'But later you changed it, claiming he was gone for over five and up to ten minutes.' I held my breath, not answering for a split-second. *Are they trying to make me look like a liar?* I asked myself. I thought back to the day spent at the parachute centre. With the kids keeping us busy, Emile had taken April to the bathroom and with him had gone the parachute.

'In the statements, what I said was an extreme reaction,' I told him, knowing there was no way for me to know for sure just how long Emile had been gone. 'I was angry when I found out about his affairs and I was out for blood. I made it sound worse because I was humiliated.'

'Was anything you said untrue?' he pushed.

'I don't think I lied,' I replied, trying to remember the state I was in at the time of the investigation. 'I just painted a worse picture, which I think anyone would do in my situation. It was the worst possible time. I had just been informed that everything I had been suspicious of was a reality and I was just out of hospital, on medication, and the red mist came down,' I added, almost worried I was being unfair to Emile by suggesting he was in the toilet longer than necessary. I wasn't trying to protect Emile, but I didn't want to sway the jury against him either. I just wanted the truth to come out, whatever it might be. 'I was gunning for him in the interview, but I did feel I brought out everything and anything. I despised him for what he had done to our family.'

'How long do you think he was in the toilet for?' the lawyer asked, and I paused. I visualized the scenario – we had just rented the kit out and Ben was lying on the mats by reception. *I went to check on them*, I remembered, having wondered why they were taking so long.

'I'd said two minutes in the first interview and over five in the second,' I replied in a sigh, trying to think it through. 'It was probably somewhere in the middle of that.' Satisfied with my answer, the lawyer turned his attention to a video that he played for the jury and I fell into silence. I stood there, watching a demonstration by an instructor carrying out a sabotage on a parachute within the confines of a Netheravon toilet cubicle. *It took him just over five minutes*, I noted, surprised by how quickly the damage was done. When the video finished, the room's attention was back on me.

'How qualified are you in skydiving?' the prosecuting lawyer asked me.

'I'm an advanced free-fall instructor,' I answered. 'So very qualified.'

'And how many jumps have you completed?' he continued.

'Around 2,600.'

'So in your expertise, what do you think could have happened with the main parachute?'

'With the main parachute . . .' I paused, thinking about how tangled and knotted it had been. 'It could have been a packing issue.'

'What are the chances of that happening?' the lawyer quizzed. 'Of a main parachute failing?'

'From what I know . . .' I hesitated, racking my brains. 'In about one in every 750 jumps, the main parachute fails.'

'What about the chances of a reserve parachute failing as well?' he pushed, and I held my breath, knowing the answer.

'One in a million,' I replied. The weight of this revelation felt like a kick to the stomach. I looked around the room, trying to focus on my parents sitting along the other side. Near them was a row of journalists, scribbling down everything that was being said. Suddenly, the whole thing seemed surreal. *Just get through it*, I told myself, thinking about the prospect of picking up April and Ben after all of this was over.

The questions turned to my marriage with Emile, and I had no choice but to tell the brutal truth: the relationship had deteriorated.

'Everything seemed to be going relatively well until around November 2014,' I admitted. 'Emile went skiing for a long period, and when he came back home it was all a bit strained. It had been for quite a while, and eventually he said he wasn't happy and wasn't sure what he wanted. I felt like we had grown in different directions.' The barrister nodded at my response before having a binder of paperwork placed in front of me. *What's this for?* I wondered, looking down at the stacks of paper inside. I flipped through what I realized were thousands of text messages from Emile's phone. I glanced through them, feeling sicker and sicker the more I read.

*Will you call me your Mr Grey?* Emile had messaged Stefanie. *I guess sometimes I will have to obey you*, she had replied. Scanning through the texts, it became apparent Emile was planning a life with Stefanie. *I will sacrifice and give up so much for you, I just never want to let you go*, he had promised her. *From April onwards I can do random and spontaneous. To be with you, I would do anything.*

The last part felt like ringing in my ears. *Why from April onwards?* I asked myself, knowing the accident had happened the first weekend of April.

When the questioning started again I tried to ignore the messages in front of me, willing myself to focus on what was happening, but I couldn't help but read through some of the texts. Emile had even messaged her from my hospital bedside. *Vicky was in tears last night saying all she could think of is she didn't say goodbye to the kids,* he had written about me. *She's undergoing surgery right now, one day we might have a family of our own.* Seeing his lack of emotion about my injuries made me want to cry.

Even more callously, at the same time he was messaging Stefanie, Emile was also making plans with Carly. *So tonight,* he had written to his ex-wife, *we fuck twice.* Seeing the betrayal in black and white was a kick in the teeth and only made me feel worse about what had happened. *I was heavily pregnant with Ben when he sent that,* I noted. Knowing Carly had gone behind my back somehow felt even worse than Emile's affair with Stefanie. I didn't know whether she got some sort of sick satisfaction from it because her own marriage to Emile hadn't worked out, but seeing the messages she had sent to him was crushing. *How could she do that to her children, to me and to my kids?* I wondered, second-guessing everything I had thought was true.

To top it all off, Emile had even been texting Stefanie while I was in labour with Ben. *I was giving birth to our son,* I thought, shattered. *And he was messaging another woman.* It was an overwhelming betrayal. Hearing the lawyer speak, I snapped back into the present.

'What did you know of Emile's money troubles over the years?'

'He had a lot of problems with money. I had given him a lot but he never paid me back,' I answered, pushing the binder to one side.

'How much money have you given to Emile?' the lawyer continued.

'Um . . .' I hesitated, adding it all up. 'Over several years I loaned him £18,000, but he had also built up debts with loan sharks.'

'Why did you write Emile out of your will?' he questioned. I paused. When it had come to buying our house with my grandmother's inheritance, I hadn't wanted Emile anywhere near the money.

'Because I couldn't trust him financially,' I replied honestly. 'I wanted to give the children some security for the future – I wasn't sure I could do that if Emile had access to it.'

'Do you suspect Emile could have tried to murder you for financial gain?'

'No, at no point would I have suspected him,' I answered. 'Emile has his faults but to an extent he loves me, and he would have at least considered the children. I know doing something to me would hurt them for the rest of their lives and, despite everything, Emile is an amazing father. I don't believe he would do that to the kids.'

With that, the court was adjourned for the day and I breathed a sigh of relief. Getting down from the stand, I looked at the time and realized I had been questioned for four hours.

'God,' I muttered to myself, making my way back to my car. *This week is going to be exhausting.* On the drive home, my parents were both quiet and subdued. A sliver of guilt crept into my mind. I knew they wanted to support me, but I had struggled to talk to them about the issues between Emile and me over the years. Instead of confiding in anyone, I had kept a lot of it hidden in the hope that things would improve. I was paying back my brother, so I had kept him protected financially. When Dad and Frances had listened to it all laid out at the trial, it must have come as a shock, and I knew hearing everything in excruciating detail was difficult for them to deal with. Picking the kids up on the way, I threw my arms around my babies.

'Mummy!' April squealed. 'Look.' She thrust a hand-drawn picture in my face.

'That's amazing,' I cooed, forcing myself to smile. *I have to pretend everything is normal for them*, I told myself, taking them home to start preparations on dinner. By the time both kids were bathed and in bed, I was drained. I lay down on my bed, mulling over the day's events. *I have to do it all again tomorrow.* I had no idea how I was going to find the energy. I grabbed my phone from the bedside table and flicked through the articles before landing on one. *Wife in parachute trial 'wanted revenge' on husband*, the headline read. *Victoria Cilliers wanted to 'cast suspicion' after giving differing*

*accounts of her husband's actions throughout the two-
year investigation.* Without thinking, I clicked onto the
comments at the bottom of the article. *Is she mad?* one
commenter wrote. *What is wrong with her?* I turned off
my phone and threw it to the other side of the bed. That
night, I struggled to sleep and it felt as though the weight
of the case rested on me.

The next morning, I quickly finished my coffee before
ferrying the kids out of the door. We acted out the same
routine, dropping April and Ben off before heading to
court. Along with Nikki, who accompanied me to the
trial every day, I also met a witness support worker
named Rochelle. She had a calm demeanour and her
stories were a welcome distraction from the reality of
being in court each day.

'How did you meet Emile Cilliers?' was the first question from the prosecution barrister that morning.

'We worked at the same gym,' I told the room, glancing over at Emile in his spot behind the glass. 'He was a
physical training instructor and I was a physio in the
gym. I got to know him a bit better because he had a
skiing accident and I treated him for a while.'

They asked about what life was like at the start of our
relationship, before the questions turned back to Emile's
behaviour after his ski trip.

'I loved him and our family but he had asked me to
wait, heavily pregnant, not knowing if he was going to
stay with us,' I told the lawyer. 'That was incredibly hard.'

'How did Emile make you feel at this point?'

'I felt scared,' I confessed. 'I was quite panicky because everything seemed to be going pear-shaped and I didn't understand why. I didn't know what I had done wrong or why he didn't want to be with me any more.'

'What about the argument when you found out Emile had been smoking in your car?' the lawyer continued. *God*, I thought. *They're really going through everything*. I had forgotten I had told police about that particular row.

'The look Emile gave me when I told him straight was incredible,' I replied, remembering just how badly he had treated me. 'He looked absolutely livid, almost blank. I hadn't seen that sort of expression before.'

'Did you feel like he wanted to leave the marriage?' he asked me.

'Sometimes, yes,' I responded. 'I felt like I was living on a time bomb, not knowing if at any point he might turn around and decide he's going.'

'So why did you cut Emile out of your will?' he continued, and I sighed. *Why do we have to go over everything again?* I wondered.

'Like I said yesterday, Emile was terrible with money and I didn't trust him as a beneficiary,' I told the court. 'After the accident I was due to receive an insurance payout, and Emile wanted to use it to pay for a trip to South Africa and for his car to be serviced. That made me so angry. After all the money I had wasted on him, I wanted to use this to stay at home with the children and spend more time recovering, not have his car serviced.'

'Did Emile know you had rewritten your will?'

'Yes, it was agreed because the money we used for the house I had inherited from my grandmother, and Emile knew that meant the children would get the house.' I paused for a moment, thinking over the post-nuptial agreement.

Then the focus shifted to Emile's affairs, and I listened to excruciating details about the sex clubs and swingers group he had frequented. *That's not the Emile I knew*, I thought to myself, in complete shock at how much he had been hiding from me. I'd had suspicions before that he had tried to quash, but for him to be masking that much was astounding. It wasn't just the odd occasion as I had suspected.

'Were you suspicious of Emile's infidelity?' the lawyer asked me, and I thought back to how protective Emile had been over his phone.

'A little bit, yes,' I acknowledged. 'The messages he got from other women didn't seem appropriate and some of his excuses didn't really ring true. He was constantly on his phone, it was ridiculous. I wasn't allowed anywhere near it, he even took it to the toilet and that made me suspicious.' I paused before adding, 'Oh, and the fact that he had started to not wear his wedding ring.'

When court was adjourned for the day, I made my way swiftly home, picking up the kids as I went. Once through the door, I kicked off my shoes, noticing the pile of unread post by the door. I scooped it up, sifting through the envelopes until I found one that caught my eye. *Victoria Cilliers, Amesbury* was all the front of the letter read. *That's odd*, I thought, tearing it open. *Whoever sent it doesn't know my full address.* I pulled out the letter and my stomach dropped. *How can you stand up for this guy?* the handwritten note read. *What are you thinking?* Along with it were several newspaper clippings, with the descriptions of Emile's actions highlighted. I put the letter to one side and, with my hands shaking, I dialled the number of my liaison officer.

'We'll get a camera installed by the front door,' he tried to reassure me when I told him about the note. 'But if you have any safety concerns, call 999.'

I hung up, feeling no safer than before. *If someone wants to hurt me,* I thought to myself, *they're not going to come through my front door.* I looked back at the letter, feeling violated. *I can't even be at home any more without someone telling me how to act.* No matter what – whether it was Emile, the police or members of the public – it felt as though I couldn't escape someone else trying to control me.

'Why did you change your statement about the length of time Emile spent in the hangar toilet?' the defence barrister asked once I was back in court. Giving evidence felt like a never-ending nightmare.

'Because I had expanded on the truth,' I replied, exhausted by the constant cross-examining.

'Why did you expand on the truth?'

'I knew it was a key point, and at that point, I wanted Emile to suffer,' I answered. *Does it matter?* I wanted to add. 'I wanted to cast suspicion on him because I had been ridiculed.' The barrister moved to the screen by my stand, and I waited for her to select one of the police tapes from my interviews.

'I'm going to play back one of the tapes for the jury,' she commented before the video started.

'Deep down I did not want to do the jump,' I watched myself say on the screen. 'But I knew I had to in order to be sure I didn't want to jump again. I had been up most of the night and by the time I got on the aircraft that morning, I was in tears for most of the ride. When I jumped out I was absolutely terrified, which was hard for me to admit because it was something I had done thousands of times. I just did not want to be there any more.' The defence barrister stood up and walked towards me.

'Why were you scared of jumping that day?' she asked me.

'I had just had a baby and I was worried about my future in the sport,' I replied. 'The jump was a test of my will to continue as an instructor, but it was to be my last one so I could focus on my family.'

'Do you think that Emile sabotaged your parachute?' she asked me.

'I don't know,' I admitted. 'Everything I knew was a lie and now I don't know. I'd still find it hard to comprehend if he did do it.' I paused, trying to imagine a scenario where Emile would hurt me. 'My gut instinct says there is no way he would do something like that to me, but I just don't know any more.' The entire experience had been painful and stressful. After four long days of standing as a witness, I was completely drained.

'You don't remember?' Elizabeth Marsh, the defence lawyer, said with a tone of disbelief. She had asked about the small details leading up to the jump and, hearing her tone, I felt stupid.

'No, I don't,' I snapped back, feeling judged for not remembering. 'You're asking me about something that happened years ago.' I felt like I was the one on trial and, after being on my feet for such a long period of time, I was exhausted.

'When you drafted the post-nuptial agreement, did Emile challenge you in any way or seek to get his name on the mortgage deed?' Ms Marsh continued.

'No, he didn't,' I responded. *Emile didn't care about anything in the end*, I added internally.

'And when you proposed the agreement, did Emile say, "that's outrageous"?'

'No, we discussed it,' I answered. 'He admitted that money was potentially an issue and, given that we anticipated being married for life, it didn't make a difference.'

'Emile had paid for life insurance, is that right?' the barrister asked.

'Yes, he had,' I replied. My legs were starting to stiffen under the strain of standing for so long.

'And where does that money go should you die?' the defence lawyer quizzed me.

'It would go to Emile,' I told her.

'Actually, that's not true. The insurance policy makes it plain that payment would go to a legal representative or executor and not necessarily to a spouse,' she interjected. 'So if Emile had died during the currency of this policy, money would have gone to his estate. Similarly, if you died the money would not go to your husband, it would go to your estate – did you know that?'

'No,' I admitted, rubbing my fingers across my temples. The weight of information had sparked a headache. 'I assumed wrongly that it went to him. I can't recall a conversation with my solicitor, I think because I thought it went to Emile. I left the house to the children in the will, knowing he would get the life insurance money.'

'Putting the insurance money aside, Emile would have been better off with you alive than you dead, wouldn't he?' she suggested. I thought about Emile's debts and how much he financially relied on me.

'Yes,' I replied. 'I suppose he would.' Satisfied with my answer, Elizabeth Marsh turned her attention to the day of the jump.

'Today, forget what anybody else has told you,' she said. 'Today, what do you say happened when you went up in that plane?'

'I just wanted to get straight out,' I replied, thinking back to the Sunday morning I had spent in the hangar. 'I didn't talk to anyone because I was quite tired and emotional. I just put my goggles and my helmet on and put my head down. The jump master decided to do three passes – I may have been nominated for the last pass but I can't remember. I do remember the pilot giving me a smile as I went out. Usually that's the part I love, the cold rush, the smell, and it just didn't hit me. I pulled the parachute and knew immediately it wasn't right. There were a lot of twists, which I got rid of, but it didn't feel right.'

'What was your thought process when you discovered the main parachute was twisted?' Ms Marsh asked me.

'I don't really understand what my thought process was at the time,' I admitted. With the trauma, my memories of the fall were patchy. 'I didn't want to be there and I did not want to be under that parachute. I cut it away but on deploying the reserve I knew that, too, was not right. The world went a little bit pear-shaped. The spin was going one way and the twists were opposite. It took quite a while to get that initial purchase. I expected everything to settle down when I got rid of all of the twists but it didn't, it just got worse. I couldn't figure out how to slow it down, it was just getting faster and faster and faster. The speed was unreal from the spin and there was just a big sort of bang and then black.'

'You had made comments about being suicidal to Emile in the past. How were you feeling on the day of the jump?' the lawyer asked.

'I was very emotional and upset but not suicidal,' I retorted.

'Did you do anything either accidentally or intentionally to manipulate your parachute?' the lawyer pushed.

'No,' I snapped back.

The day had all but drained the life out of me but, when my part in the trial was finally over, I tried my best to get on with everyday life. *I just want to push it all to the back of my mind for now*, I thought to myself, but it felt as though I wasn't allowed to. In the mornings I'd take April to school, but peering through my curtains I'd usually spot at least one reporter lingering by my door. I sighed.

'We've got to be quiet,' I told April, leading her through the back garden to my car, which I had purposely parked round the corner. When people started looking through my windows, I threw net curtains and blinds up around the house, desperate for some level of privacy. Intermittently, unsolicited post arrived at the door, sometimes handwritten, sometimes typed. *What is wrong with you?* they wrote in anger. *Your husband is evil and you're stupid if you don't see that*. That comment brought me to a stop at the kitchen counter and I held my breath until I was sure I wasn't going to cry. *You're telling me he's evil*, I imagined saying back to them. *Yet you're the one sending me sinister notes.*

I felt unsafe, like there was a massive and unwanted spotlight on me. As the trial progressed, old friends began to sell stories about me, and the photographer who had shot mine and Emile's wedding photos sold them to the press. Each incident felt like a betrayal and all of it added to my increasing isolation. I felt trapped in my home, not knowing who to trust, so I trusted no one.

Over the next couple of weeks, I kept my eye on the media reports and, listening to the news one evening, I heard how Emile had suggested a stranger had tried to kill me.

'Victoria's evidence is that it is inconceivable that this was an accident, and you agree, don't you?' Michael Bowes, the prosecuting barrister, had said to him. Emile had agreed. 'So the notion of a complete stranger trying to sabotage a parachute track with the sudden urge to kill someone, without knowing who it belonged to, is ridiculous.'

'It's a possibility,' Emile had replied.

'It's also a possibility a number of asteroids will strike the earth, isn't it?' Mr Bowes had retorted. It came out in the press that Emile had admitted in a police interview that there had been little chance of me surviving the fall and, as more details came to light, the news bulletins were endless. One article read, *Cilliers had been planning to leave his wife for weeks before the near-fatal fall.*

One night, morbid curiosity got the better of me and, without thinking, I searched my name on Google. Scrolling past the list of articles, I found online chat rooms that were discussing the trial. *Victoria Cilliers is the scum of the earth*, one nasty comment read. *She deserves everything she got.* I quickly clicked away from the page, feeling sick. It felt like the story had become so warped by now that people were forming opinions based on the almost pantomime presentation that the media had portrayed. *But that's not our life at all*, I thought. From reading just one or two articles, these people believed they knew me and understood what I had been through, but they had no idea.

After six weeks, the trial was coming to a close and the jurors were sent to deliberate. But before long, reports of bullying in the jury deliberations were also in the press. Keen to know what was happening at court, I switched on the TV that evening and turned it to a news channel.

'Today in the parachute murder trial,' the newsreader began, 'two jurors have been discharged after the High Court judge, Mr Justice Sweeney, was provided with medical certificates as accusations of bullying plague the jury.' I shook my head in disbelief before searching my phone for articles on the matter, only to find that the jurors had been let off due to stress. *What the hell? You think you're stressed?* I raged to myself. *Try living this for years, I'll show you what fucking stress is.* I was livid, knowing that the jury members could go home at the end of the day to their families. It was just a few weeks of their lives, when it had been years of mine, and that infuriated me. All I wanted was this awful saga in my life to end but, scrolling through the online media, as I did every evening, I was stopped dead in my tracks.

*After eight days of deliberation in skydive attempted murder case, judge orders a retrial.* I read the headline over and over again. *No, that can't be right.* I scrolled through the article and, to my horror, I discovered the trial had collapsed. *Today jurors passed a note to the judge, stating they would be unable to reach a verdict.*

*Are you fucking joking?* I choked in shock. *After all of this?* I couldn't believe what I was reading. *How many more months do I have to wait?* I wondered. The time frame just kept being extended, over and over again. In the last two and a half years, I had lost my husband, my social life, my privacy. All of that was gone. Meanwhile, everything was unknown: who to believe, what to believe, what had really happened that fateful day. But what remained unchanged was that I was stuck, trapped in a nightmare with no idea when or how it was going to end.

*The retrial is expected to take place around Easter next year*, the article said. *That's five months away*, I thought. *Five more months of my life taken away.*

# 13

# Retrial

*I suppose at least I'll know what to expect this time*, I thought as I geared myself up for the retrial. *So that's one positive to come out of the last trial.* The date had been set for 11 April 2018, but I was not due to stand as a witness until several weeks after that. While I waited for the ordeal to begin again, I tried to carry on as best as I could, focusing on April and Ben. April still remembered Emile and frequently asked about him. Ben, on the other hand, seemed none the wiser that someone was missing from the house.

Although I just wanted to be left alone to fix my broken family, I couldn't help but keep a close eye on the news. *Parachute murder bid accused appeals for bail conditions to be amended*, the headlines read a few weeks after Emile's trial had collapsed. I was stunned to discover Emile was back at Winchester Crown Court, this time asking if he could spend a month in South Africa with his parents.

'He resides in the barracks,' Elizabeth Marsh, his defence lawyer, had said. 'There won't be many people there because he's in a training unit, and there'll be no training over Christmas.' *Is it safe to let him travel to South Africa?* I wondered to myself. Emile had been granted permission to travel to Europe in a sporting competition while awaiting the first trial, but I knew he had been under strict conditions and an army supervisor had held on to Emile's passport. *If he's allowed to go to Cape Town, he might not come back.* I scanned through the reports, searching for the outcome.

'I have concluded that I will not alter the bail conditions,' the judge decided. 'They will remain as they are.' Seeing his appeal denied, I breathed a slight sigh of relief. I wanted an end to the limbo I was stuck in, and if Emile absconded I'd never get a resolution.

When the first day of the trial finally arrived, I once again couldn't help but look up what had been happening in court. Given I had already spent days on the witness stand and weeks poring over the news, I thought there was nothing unpleasant left that I hadn't already heard about Emile, but seeing the new reports, I was stunned. *They're going in much harder this time*, I realized, reading through articles fresh from the trial. *The court heard today that Cilliers arranged to have sex with a prostitute in the weeks before the near-fatal fall*, one said.

'This is a man who cared absolutely nothing for his wife and treated her with absolute contempt,' prosecuting lawyer Michael Bowes was quoted as saying. 'He wanted to be rid of her and wanted to live his own life on his terms. He cared nothing for her, and in truth, only cared for himself. He had decided to get rid of her permanently.' I felt numb reading the court quotes.

I thought the original trial had prepared me for what was to come, but this time I was on the stand for even longer. On my first day in the witness box the video recording of my first police interview began to play.

'As soon as I pulled the parachute I knew something wasn't right, I was fighting against the canopy as it spun out of control,' I watched myself say. I looked at my face, worn out from the ordeal. In the police station I was sitting in front of the camera wearing a body brace with a crutch under each arm. *I look completely broken*, I noted. I'd seen the video at the first trial but it was still shocking to be reminded about the extent of my own injuries.

'How experienced was Emile at skydiving?' the detective had asked me.

'He's less experienced than I am,' I had replied. 'He's only completed around 200 jumps, but he does know how to pack a parachute. He has worked as a parachute packer, packing people's parachutes. I taught him how to pack them.' The court listened to Michael Bowes describe the course Emile had been on before the accident.

'He part-completed a course in reserve parachute packing,' the lawyer explained. 'And while he never finished the full assessment, he had done enough to give him the knowledge to tamper with one if he wanted to.' *That's true*, I agreed, before my attention was turned back to the police interview. The recording began to play again and, painfully, I listened to myself in despair.

'Emile said he wasn't happy any more,' I had told the police. 'He was having a mid-life crisis and he wasn't sure if he wanted that sort of relationship any more. I know he was talking to a counsellor-type person to address what he was feeling, because he was adamant that he didn't want to call time on our relationship without investigating what he wanted.' Following more questioning, the prosecution went on to read out a note I had left in my will for Emile to find, in case he would attempt to claim money after I had died.

'Dear executors,' the lawyer read aloud. 'In the event of my death, I would like to leave my estate to my children. By his own admission, Emile poorly manages money and I am not confident the money I leave would be used for the benefit of the children. I do hope, Emile, that you understand my reasoning. I love you and you are an amazing father.' Listening to the note, I felt tears prick my eyes, aware of Emile hearing this at the other end of the room. But there was no privacy left for me in the trial. The prosecution dragged out the sordid details of Emile's affairs and it was humiliating on all counts. They also quizzed me endlessly on the events after I had left the plane, trying to figure out if I had cut away a good parachute. By then my confidence was so low that the idea I might have misjudged my situation didn't seem impossible.

'Ultimately, I don't know if the main parachute was

good,' I admitted, not wanting to commit to something I couldn't even remember. 'I know the lines were twisted but it happened years ago. I've got very patchy memories of the incident and I just can't picture it.' Most of the things I had remembered came from flashbacks in the weeks after the fall.

'What about the time Emile spent in the hangar toilet,' the lawyer pushed. 'How long do you think he was in there for?'

'I've explained this a hundred times over, but I don't know,' I replied, frustrated. 'It could have been a couple of minutes, it could have been five.'

'Why did you change your statement?'

'Because I was angry,' I retorted. 'My whole world had just been blown apart in front of me. I don't know how long it was.' Throughout my appearance in court I couldn't help the growing niggling feeling I had. *What if he did it?* I wondered, aware how much my evidence was helping his defence. *What if I say something wrong and he's let off, or spends only a few years in prison – where does that leave me?* I was feeling stronger mentally by now, more able to accept that Emile could be guilty. But if Emile was guilty that made me his target and I was terrified of what Emile was capable of doing. As the lawyers pushed me, it felt like I was being backed into a corner. *You're asking me to give evidence but I don't know what the consequences of that will be*, I thought. *If refusing to condemn my husband keeps me alive, then I'll do it*, I told myself, thinking of April and Ben. I was ready to do anything in my power to stay alive for them.

At the end of a gruelling day, I left court to return home. I picked up the children and had to pretend nothing was wrong. I put on a facade for them but inside I was a wreck. *What does their future look like?* I asked myself, watching them play together before bedtime. *How will this affect them?* I tucked them into bed that night, wearily knowing that the process would start all over again the next day.

I couldn't decide who was tougher on me, the defence or the prosecution. This time the evidence pack I was given had every text message Emile sent, rather than the redacted version I saw at the first trial. I think the prosecution wanted to shock me with the brutal reality of his infidelities. Both sides questioned me for hours on end, tirelessly trying to pull apart my memories from the incident.

'In your initial statement, were you telling the truth?' Michael Bowes asked me for what felt like the hundredth time. I took a deep breath.

'I elaborated,' I replied, worn out from the constant scrutiny.

'Were you telling the truth?' he pushed.

'No,' I stated simply. I glanced around the room, feeling every eye on me, and it felt like each person was judging me.

'So what you're telling the jury, then, is that when you made that statement you lied?' the lawyer continued to press, and I sighed. *Do I really have to go over this again?*

'I'm not saying I lied completely but, as I have said before, I was angry and I elaborated throughout the statement to paint Emile in a bad light,' I explained once again. 'I know what I said in my police statement, and I had a reason and a motive for doing that. I was angry when the police interviewed me.' *After all, I had just found out that he was definitively having an affair.* Finally satisfied with my answer, the lawyer shifted his line of questioning to the day before the fall, reminding me of the statement I had previously made to police about the time Emile had spent in the toilet with my parachute.

'Today, are you concerned about the amount of time Cilliers spent in the toilet with the parachute?' Mr Bowes asked.

'No, I'm not,' I responded, thinking back to the day he was referring to. *I have answered this so many times*, I thought, remembering Emile taking April to the toilet, the parachute swung over his shoulder. *For the life of me, I cannot remember how long he took.*

'That's not what you told police during your interviews,' the lawyer retorted, snapping me back into reality. I held my breath, feeling stuck. *I was concerned and angry then*, I replied internally. I had explained my reasoning so many times and it was frustrating that the lawyers still didn't seem to understand. *Is this ever going to end?* I wondered.

When it came to Emile's questioning, I wasn't allowed

in the room and I didn't want to be. I simply wanted to return to my own world with the children. Of course, that was easier said than done. Each day that the trial continued, my anxiety ran through the roof. The years of wanting answers, of living in a strange bubble while I waited for Emile to be found innocent or guilty, were about to end. Either verdict would affect my life. If he was found guilty, my children would be forced to live with the stigma of having a father in prison, and I would feel further humiliated by the media portrayal of me as a dupe who stuck by him. If he was found innocent, I would need to find a way to co-parent with him and manage some kind of relationship. And I had the added worry that he might be guilty but set free to try to kill me again. As the possibilities spun in my brain, I relied on the news to relay what had been said.

'Did you harbour any wish to harm your wife or the children?' his defence lawyer asked Emile.

'No, never,' Emile replied. 'I would never do anything to harm any of them.' The news reported on an all-inclusive holiday Emile had gone on with his girlfriend. I looked at the dates. *I was pregnant with Ben at that point*, I noted to myself with a sinking heart. *He'd left me at home on my own to have fun with her.*

'I knew I couldn't afford it,' Emile said about the holiday. 'I was being stupid and I wasn't thinking properly.' The text messages between them were printed in black and white. *I might leave my job*, Emile had told her. *And then we can be together.*

'Were you really considering leaving your job?' Ms Marsh asked Emile.

'No,' he replied. 'I was merely stringing Stefanie along. I was unhappy in my relationship with Vicky. I think we got married too soon, but I'd planned to stay with her until the baby was six weeks old. Then I was going to make a decision.'

The total lack of concern for me was obvious. The media reported on how financially unstable Emile was and, reading the articles, I felt embarrassed. *Court hears how wife in parachute murder trial was a 'cash cow'*. I clicked away from the news site, unable to read any more. *I'm being made to look like a mug*, I thought. Meanwhile, Emile's defence was focusing on how much he had stolen from me.

'Emile was no Prince Charming,' Ms Marsh told the court. 'But killing Victoria would be the equivalent of killing the goose that lays the golden egg.' *Well, that's just great,* I scoffed. *That's all I was to him.* The court heard how Emile spent his money, wasting thousands of pounds on unnecessary items. When I saw the details, I gasped. *£3,500 for a TV,* I read. *What for?* Other expenses included electronic gadgets, skiing equipment and clothes, which he hoarded either in our garage or at the army barracks. *He didn't even put most of it to use,* I thought, realizing how compulsive his spending had been.

'He lied to fuel his lust and cover his erratic financial tracks, but his lies were mainly flights of fancy,' his lawyer said, defending him.

At last, nearly seven months since the original trial began, and over three years since the fall, the jury were sent to deliberate. The hours waiting for their decision were tense – in that pocket of time, my entire life hung in the balance. The way Emile had treated me was appalling but I still couldn't totally picture him as a murderer. Right then I felt that a 'not guilty' verdict would be enough confirmation for me to believe he was innocent in all of this, that my nightmares were just that – fears conjured out of my mind. I held my breath, refreshing my phone over and over again each day, waiting to hear the result. Finally, the jury were called back into court. I had decided not to wait around for the verdict, having spent enough time in court. Instead, I went back to work to distract myself by keeping busy – but now I was desperately anxious to know what was happening.

After repeatedly refreshing my phone, an article popped up. *Emile Cilliers found guilty on two counts of attempted murder.* I froze. *Is that right?* I rushed to the TV and turned on the news. There on the screen was a detective I recognized from the investigation.

'I don't think we can underestimate the ordeal Victoria has been put through,' he told the cameras. 'She has been made to give evidence twice, and again on top of all the physical and emotional trauma she suffered from that horrendous fall, where it is only a miracle really that she survived. Physically she is well, but obviously she is still traumatized and there is a long way for her to go. It's a very difficult time for her, and has been and will continue for a while, I would imagine. I think the real danger with Emile Cilliers is he is cold, calculated, what he did was deliberate and done for financial and sexual motives, and there was absolutely no consideration of his wife or anyone else. He serves his own needs and that makes him a very dangerous man in my opinion.' The image switched to a newsreader.

'Emile Cilliers showed no emotion as he was convicted unanimously on two counts of attempted murder and was also found guilty on a third count of recklessly endangering life.' I reached for the remote and turned off the screen.

Even though I'd been waiting for the verdict, I was still stunned by how life seemed to have turned so suddenly. I took some time off work to try to get my head round it all, but it didn't really help. I was also careful not to watch the news in front of the kids, scared in case a clip about Emile popped up and April recognized him.

A few days after the conviction, my phone pinged with a text message. I glanced at the screen and saw it was from Emile's mum in South Africa. *Emile is devastated by the verdict*, she wrote. *He still loves you.* I stood still, not knowing what to say. It felt as though no matter who I spoke to, I was being guilted into taking a side. Some of my friends wanted me to despise Emile, yet here was his mother wanting me to forgive him.

\* \* \*

It was after the verdict that I was finally allowed to speak to Emile myself. *I have to*, I thought to myself as I prepared for a phone call from prison. *I need closure.* I didn't know what to expect and I was apprehensive, having imagined for three years what this conversation would be like. I thought I would cry or shout but, when the phone rang and I picked it up, I didn't feel anything.

'Hi Vicky.' Emile's familiar voice broke the silence.

'Hello,' I replied. I thought about all the things I could say, all of the hurtful things he had done to me, but by now so much time had passed.

'So, how are you?' he asked. *This is bizarre*, I thought.

'I'm fine,' I answered. I didn't speak much, telling him briefly about the kids and where they were at in life.

'I still don't know what's going on,' Emile told me. 'But my lawyers say I need to prepare for a harsh sentence.'

'Right,' I replied, at a loss for what to say. Before we hung up the phone, Emile asked if I would visit him in prison. 'I'll have to think about it,' I told him honestly. Afterwards, I mulled the conversation over in my mind. *I can't end things like this*, I decided. *I have too many questions.*

I arrived at Winchester Prison with countless pages of questions that I had written out in a notebook.

'You can't take that in with you,' a guard said, stopping me.

'Oh,' I replied, stumped. 'It's just a list of things I want to say.' I tried to reason with him but the guard shook his head, and so I had no choice but to hand over the notebook. Walking into the room to see Emile waiting for me was surreal. It was as though I recognized him but it wasn't quite the same man any more.

'Hi,' I said bluntly, taking the chair opposite. His face looked worn and older than I remembered. I immediately started with my questions, racking my brains, trying to remember what I had written down. I asked him about items that had gone missing from the house, which I assumed he'd sold, but he denied that he'd taken them. I asked him about his infidelities but couldn't really get an answer.

'It wasn't your fault,' he repeated over and over again.

'Did you try to hurt me with the parachute and gas?' I asked outright. *I need to hear it from him*, I thought to myself.

'No.' Emile shook his head before burying it in his hands. 'I'm innocent.'

I watched him cry and realized that I still didn't know if I believed him or not, but I wasn't sure I cared either way. It was hard to see him in these surroundings. The Emile I had fallen in love with was charming and charismatic. He had been well respected in the army and to see him now, with his scruffy hair and prison tracksuit on, felt like a fall from grace. He was a broken man. Leaving the prison, I felt a mixture of relief and sorrow. *Regardless of what happens now,* I thought on the drive home, *I know our marriage is over.* Whilst I was still battling to completely accept that the fall had been his fault, there was no denying the strings of affairs, the constant lies and sneaking around. He'd had no respect for me and I didn't want to live like that any more. I realized that bit by bit, almost without me noticing, life had been getting easier and I had started enjoying it again.

For the sentencing, I had been granted permission to sit in the courtroom. I took my place, waiting as everyone began to pile in. The room was full of people whispering and lawyers murmuring to one another, but everyone fell silent as the judge entered and began his summing-up of the case. As he spoke I didn't look at Emile, conscious of all the journalists present who were watching me, waiting for a reaction. It was only now in the courtroom, hearing every unpleasant fact read out in its entirety, that the gravity of what Emile had done hit me properly for the first time. Each detail regarding Emile's behaviour was more damning than the last: the lying, the stealing, his complete disregard for me. *He's a monster*, I understood.

'Emile is a danger to the public,' the judge concluded. 'This was wicked offending of extreme gravity.' He paused, turning to face Emile. 'Your offending was extremely serious. There were two attempts to murder your wife. They were planned and carried out in cold blood for your own selfish purposes, which include financial gain. You have shown yourself to be a person of quite exceptional callousness who will stop at nothing to satisfy his own desires, material or otherwise. Nor have you shown the slightest sign of remorse. That your wife survived at all was miraculous. She undoubtedly suffered severe physical harm and must have suffered psychological harm both in the terror of the fall and since. She appears to have recovered from her physical injuries but not, having seen her in the witness box at great length, from the psychological harm.' I held my breath for the sentencing, knowing it wasn't going to be light. 'You will serve a minimum of eighteen years behind bars.'

I left the room, still without so much as glancing at Emile, and headed for the door. Outside, I knew the press would be a flurry of snapping cameras and pointed questions, so I made sure to slip out through a back exit. I fled the court unnoticed, escaping the mess Emile had created. Meeting up with one of my friends, Helen, who had come to support me, we headed out to have a drink in a local pub. I felt numb, completely stunned by the outcome, but Helen listened as I talked, and chatted away when I needed a distraction. *I don't want to think about it any more*, I thought. *I don't even want to address it.*

Once again in the safety of my own home, I reached for my phone to see what had been said. The articles were swirling. *Dangerous, coercive and manipulative* was how they described Emile, and I couldn't disagree any longer.

With the sentencing now behind us, I finally had the answers to April's questions.

'Listen, I need to talk to you,' I told her, sitting my little girl down on the sofa. 'It's about Daddy.'

'What about Daddy?' she puzzled, her ears pricking up at even the mention of Emile.

'You know how he isn't here any more?' I explained, and she nodded. 'Well, that's because Daddy's been bad and he's had to go to prison.' I waited for April to process that information, watching her turn to look at me, a frown wrinkling across her tiny face.

'Why?' she asked. I had the answer ready.

'Because he did something to Mummy's parachute,' I replied gently. 'And that's why I had the accident.' I knew that April had vague memories of the time I had spent in hospital and the crutches I had needed to carry around for months.

'Why did he do that?' she questioned, and I racked my brain for an explanation.

'I don't know,' I eventually said honestly. 'I don't know why he did that but he's going to be in prison for a long time.'

'OK,' she replied, before jumping in with another question. 'Can I visit him?'

'No, sweetheart,' I said, tucking a piece of hair behind her ear. 'Little children can't go into big jails.'

'Well, when am I going to see him then?' she pushed, and I quickly did the maths.

'The earliest you'll be able to see him is when you're twenty-four,' I replied, and April seemed happy with that answer. She went back to her day, playing happily with

Ben, throwing the occasional question back to me, which I answered as best I could. But over the next few months, the constant questions she had about Emile seemed to die down. She now had something to work with that she could understand and, even though she doesn't quite understand what it all really means, knowing where her father is and why she can't contact him has been the comfort she was looking for.

With Ben, things were simpler. He had no memory of Emile, only an abstract sense of an absent person he called 'Daddy'. When asked, he would say that his daddy was in jail but even then, he was too young to understand what that meant. It was important for me to be honest with the kids, especially April – she needed to know a version of the truth. At school, there would be no preventing it if another child decided to come up to them and tell them about Emile, particularly in the modern age of the internet – I knew sheltering them was futile. So instead, I decided to give them both the information necessary to make sense of Emile's absence. If they want to know more when they are older, I will tell them the whole story.

For the first few days after the sentencing there was a buzz of media interest, but quickly it started to die down and, over the summer, I was left to think about everything in my own time. Now, there was no one pushing me in any set direction. I didn't have the media or the police or social services breathing down my neck. The lawyers were gone, Emile was behind bars, and I was left to mull things over and reflect on everything.

The one confidant I knew I was able to rely on over the years was my padre, Rob. As a chaplain for the military, he approached me through the army welfare support system and offered me complete confidentiality if I ever needed someone to talk to. At a loss for where else to turn, and with a lot of my friends holding strong opinions on the case, I took him up on his offer and spoke to him regularly. It was only when talking to Rob that I felt free enough to be able to be truly honest about how I was feeling and what was going on. Knowing he was there for me at any time, day or night, helped me to keep going. He supported me throughout all of the ups and downs, which really helped me to stay balanced when I could have easily spiralled into despair.

Now, I was ready to shed the weight of the past. I had been holding on to it for so long, wishing hopelessly that one day I'd wake up and all of this would have been a nightmare. But with the sentencing behind us, I knew it was time to move on. Even though I felt ready for a fresh start, that didn't stop Emile from contacting me. After three years of not being able to speak to him, now it was like I couldn't escape him. I was bombarded with letters and phone calls from the prison. At first, I wrote back. He sounded like the old Emile, the one I met in the gym, the one who wrote me letters full of affection and love, and there was so much to say and find out. But soon the constant contact felt oppressive and the old, controlling Emile seemed to be slipping out of the woodwork. It was the first time I'd seen this control in a clear-eyed way, although it took a while for me to learn how to deal with it. He was constantly wanting me to book visits.

'I only have so much annual leave,' I tried to explain. 'I have to save time for the children.' *I can't use all of my holiday going on prison visits*, I thought, bewildered by how much he was expecting of me.

'No one else will come,' he told me. 'You're all I've got left.'

Once, I would have felt sorry for him, but no more. After weeks of pushing, it finally came to a head in a phone call one afternoon.

'I need to know the honest truth,' Emile told me. 'What do you want?'

I paused for a second, looking around me. My two beautiful children were playing happily in the living room while I was distracted, being pulled away from them by the daily phone conversations.

'I don't want this,' I admitted. 'I don't want this marriage.' I waited for a response but Emile fell quiet.

'Right,' he eventually replied. 'I have to go.' I listened to the sound of the line cutting out and I sighed. I had spent my life married to Emile in constant fear that he would leave me, but now too much had happened for me to feel any satisfaction in having the upper hand. It was a few days before he called again one afternoon.

'I've been thinking about it and I'll back off,' he announced. 'I'll give you time to decide what you want.'

'OK,' I agreed, the fear of upsetting him still so deeply ingrained I didn't point out that I'd already told him what I wanted. But over the course of the next few months, I grew stronger and stopped engaging with Emile. Realizing he wasn't getting anywhere with me, his calls tailed off at last.

Once I'd understood that the relationship was toxic, it felt like a weight had been lifted from my shoulders. Accepting that the man who was supposed to love me unconditionally was, in fact, abusive, was the most difficult thing I had ever processed. *I was trapped*, I thought, reflecting on the person I had been when Emile was around. *I don't even recognize myself.* It took escaping Emile's control to accept that he had even been controlling at all. And it took time on my own to figure out and fully accept that Emile was guilty of trying to kill me.

In the past I had been so scared of what might happen that I turned a blind eye to Emile's deceit and abuse. But I have seen just how sinister and insidious domestic abuse can be, and I have come out the other side. I'm more confident now in what I want out of life, and what I want is freedom. I want to live my life with my children by my side and be able to move on. Being free, free from Emile and his lies, feels like a second chance. He was clever in his manipulation. He wormed his way into the centre of my world and made me feel like my life revolved around him. But I've seen what life looks like without Emile and, for the first time in a long time, I'm looking forward to the future. *The relationship is over now*, I told myself. *It's time to move on.*

# 14

# Another Jump

Whenever I think about Emile now, I feel detached. The love is gone but so is the hate. There is only so long you can get caught up in an intense emotion about something like the fall. It wears you down and, at this point, I was ready to remove myself from the whole situation. It almost felt like the jump had happened to someone else.

At the same time, a sport I had loved so much had turned into a nightmare and it wasn't how I wanted to give up skydiving. Instead of choosing to leave the sport, I had been forcibly uprooted from it and, because of that, I knew I didn't want that jump to be my last. While the investigation was still ongoing I thought it would be inappropriate, but once the trial had concluded, thoughts about skydiving crept up again. *What if I did another jump?* I wondered. *Would it help me move on?* Skydiving had been such a huge part of my life for so long. *I want to end on a high*, I decided. *On a good jump.* It felt like the right time to turn the negative – all the connotations that I now associated with jumping – into a positive. When a reporter called Sarah Oliver interviewed me after the trial ended, she asked if I had any intentions of jumping again.

'I will if you will,' I smirked, challenging her.

'OK,' she immediately agreed. *Oh god*, I thought as soon as I'd said it. *I guess I have to put my money where my mouth is.* The support from Sarah and my friends around me gave me a real push. I had wanted to raise money for Wiltshire Air Ambulance. They had saved my life that day on the airfield, and doing another jump for charity felt poignant. It made sense to tie the two together. I went through all of the necessary steps, contacting my surgeon to have an assessment.

'I'm happy for you to jump,' he told me, pleased with the progress of my recovery. He signed all of the medical paperwork, so all that was left was to book a date. I knew I didn't want to do the jump at Netheravon. *It wouldn't feel right to ask them*, I decided. They had been hounded by the press during the months of the trial and it felt wrong to return there. Instead, I approached a different local parachute centre. Initially they were fine with me jumping there, but they were oddly reticent when it came to booking in the date. Nonetheless, I geared myself up for the jump, letting them know which day I wanted to do it. As the day drew closer the nerves started to kick in, but a week before I was due to jump, the parachute centre called me up.

'I'm sorry, Victoria,' a member of staff broke the news on the phone. 'But we don't think it's a good idea for you to come and jump here.'

'Oh,' I replied, disheartened. 'Why not?'

'We don't want any negative publicity,' she answered, and the let-down shocked me.

'Why would you get negative publicity?' I asked in confusion, but it was no use, the parachute centre had made up their minds. *I don't understand*, I thought after the phone call ended. *I haven't done anything wrong.* The jump was in aid of the air ambulance, a service that helps skydivers on a regular basis. The news came as an emotional blow. Skydiving was such a tight-knit community and yet the centre wanted nothing to do with me – that was what hit me the hardest. Determined to persevere, I phoned a friend who worked with the chief instructor at another parachute centre further afield.

'That sounds great, Vicky,' he reassured me as I told him my plans. 'Let me speak to the owner.' I waited for him to contact the owner of the parachute centre, and within an hour my friend called back.

'It's not a problem, just give me a date and I'll book you in.' A rush of excitement ran through me that I hadn't felt in years, followed swiftly by fear. I imagined a horror scenario where the worst happened again. *What if I'm not so lucky this time?* I felt a sinking feeling settle in my stomach as the unthinkable memories of the last jump came flooding back. *If I don't jump, I can't fall*, I thought. It seemed like an obvious solution to my worries, but cancelling the jump wouldn't put an end to the psychological torture the incident had put me through. *It's now or never*, I told myself. I wanted to jump with my friends and so it was arranged that a group of us would go up in a lift.

'I want to do a tandem jump,' I told the parachute centre over the phone. *Accidents happen*, I thought. *And I don't know if I can save myself twice*. I knew I couldn't trust myself to have the mental strength to cut away another parachute and pull the reserve, so having another diver strapped to me was the only alternative. I knew some people must have thought I was mad for organizing it, but jumping felt like the only way to reclaim my life. Everything had been so unclear for years – from the moment Emile was arrested I hadn't known what my future looked like. I needed to escape this vortex of uncertainty, and the only way to do that was to jump.

I was booked in for a Saturday morning, but by Friday afternoon the heavens had opened, and a jump was looking increasingly unlikely.

'We're postponing it until Sunday,' a friend rang me to say.

'That's fine,' I replied calmly, but inside my stomach was doing somersaults. The night before the jump, I was restless. Constant flashbacks of the incident rattled through my mind and every time I drifted off to sleep I awoke in a panicked cold sweat with my heart pounding. *This is affecting me more than I thought it would*, I realized, already willing the day to be over.

On the day of the jump, my dad arrived in Wiltshire to cheer me on along with a group of my friends. April and Ben were there too, waiting patiently to see the plane take flight.

'We're going to get you on the first lift,' I was told upon arrival, but as the day wore on, the flight continued to be delayed. Just being at a parachute centre again was difficult for me. The sounds and smells took me right back to the day of the fall, and I started to feel dizzy. *Stay focused*, I thought, urging myself to get through the day. I was doing the tandem jump with a good friend of mine, Nick, who had supported me over the years. *He'll keep us safe*, I told myself, and just the notion that I would be jumping with someone I knew and trusted helped me to calm down.

I held my nerve and, when it was finally time, I walked out to the aircraft with my head held high. I squinted up at the blue sky. It was a perfect day and the sun beamed down as I approached the open door. The slight chill of icy wind flying across the airfield was the only hint of autumn. *I can do this*, I thought, trying to psych myself up. As soon as I boarded though, I immediately began to panic. The sound of the propellers was deafening and the familiar smell of the plane started to make me feel sick. My heart rate rocketed. I tightened my goggles and strapped my helmet in place, feeling the engine roar. As we took off, tears began to roll down my cheeks and it was as though I couldn't stop it. I cried uncontrollably, growing all the more anxious as we climbed two miles into the sky. While I was used to being overlooked on the planes, no one worrying about me because I was an instructor, this flight was different. All eyes were on me, but each face was familiar and everything said to me was a gesture of reassurance.

'At the end of the day, this is entirely up to you,' Nick comforted me. 'You're going to be strapped to me the entire time, I'll look after you.' Sarah Oliver was on board as promised and she smiled at me as we made eye contact. 'Whatever you want to do, Vicky,' Nick continued. 'We'll support you.'

In a way, the total lack of pressure to jump gave me the power to do it. *This is my choice*, I recognized, realizing that now I had complete autonomy over my life. *I'm free to do what I want.* I thought back to my last jump and how much I hadn't wanted to go through with it. *I had a sixth sense that day*, I recalled. *But Emile pushed me to stay.* This time, the people who surrounded me only had my best interests at heart.

As the plane levelled, the door was lifted open and everything changed. The cold air pummelled through the aircraft and I felt different. *I want to jump.* Giving my diving partner a thumbs-up, we made our way to the exit. There was a pause for a split-second as we teetered over the edge. A layer of clouds lay underneath us and what waited for me beneath was unknown. I took a deep breath, letting my heartbeat slow down. A rush of air hit my face and, just as calmly as we had sat at the open doorway, my partner leaned forward and we fell.

*Oh my god*, I thought as we ripped through the clouds. *This is amazing.* It felt just like it used to, with the adrenaline coursing through my veins. We dropped at an accelerating rate and I could see the ground sprawled out thousands of feet beneath us. *I am completely weightless.* I looked around, smiling at the friendly faces dotted through the sky, all in free fall around me. *This feels so different*, I thought, allowing myself to let go of the pain I had been holding on to. This time I wasn't alone, all of my friends were here to experience this with me. Before I knew it, Nick tugged on the cord and our parachute billowed out above us, jolting me upright. *He's opened it sooner than I'd expected*, I thought, but realized he had probably done it so I didn't have to worry. I relaxed as our rapid plummet slowed into a controlled descent.

'We've got a good parachute,' my diving partner shouted to me, and I nodded, letting the relief sink in. In most jumps I would spin or play around, but I had told Nick that I didn't want to do that, remembering all too well the violent spins that had catapulted me to the ground three years ago. Instead we took it steady, and as we approached the drop zone, the field came into view and so did my babies.

'Mummy, Mummy!' April shouted to me, with Ben squealing by her side. The landing was textbook and, tearing off my helmet, I was greeted by enthusiastic hugs from my children. I looked over at Dad, tears forming in his eyes, and suddenly I felt emotional.

'You did it,' he congratulated, throwing his arms around me. Just like last time I was surrounded by people, but today they were cheering, celebrating what I had achieved. When Sarah came over to ask me a few questions, I was grinning from ear to ear.

'After the horror of last time,' she asked, 'what on earth possessed you to skydive again?' I laughed.

'There's a fine line between bravery and stupidity,' I told her. 'And, although I've made a fantastic physical recovery, in psychological terms, my head has still been lagging behind, and jumping was an integral part of fixing that.'

'Well, you've done yourself proud,' she replied, and I returned to the celebrations. Amongst the hugs and pats on the back, there was another poignant reason to feel accomplished today. I had agreed to do the article covering the jump in order to get some more exposure for the air ambulance. Through the press coverage and generous donations, I raised just over £5,000, and that was an amazing feeling. Repaying the paramedics for saving my life felt like another step in moving forward. *After all, they're the reason my babies have a mummy*, I recognized.

When the story went to print, I couldn't help but look through the comments. I'd been hesitant about putting myself out into the public domain again, half expecting the same vile comments I'd received in the past to resurface. But reading through what people had said, I felt positive, not finding a single negative reaction.

Now I feel free to move on with my life. The flashbacks have begun to subside and I feel excited about the future. It's as though I had to rewrite my memory of the fall. Only by jumping again was I finally free of the past. In a strange way, the charity jump has made me miss skydiving. For so long I had feared the worst that I had forgotten how incredible it felt to jump. The charity jump may or may not be my last. Who knows, perhaps when the kids are older I will take to the skies again? But for now, they are my focus.

We're working on building memories as a trio, even taking our first family holiday together. Learning to parent alone is no mean feat, and it has taken me a lot of nights crying in the shower to get it right. Sitting on the porch of our holiday home in Dorset, I feel accomplished. The kids have been tucked in and have gone to sleep without any tantrums. With the light outside still dimming, I open a bottle of wine and pour myself a glass. I watch the sunset on my own.

The future is still far from certain, but I'm learning to take joy from the unknown, and I've even started seeing someone new. Learning to open up to someone again is hard, but we are taking it slowly and he supports me unreservedly when I'm going through dark days and sleepless nights. I feel ready to take charge of my own happiness. In December 2018, I officially filed for divorce, and once it is finalized Emile will be in my past for good. It took a long time for me to see how coercive and manipulative my husband was, but I won't be controlled any longer. I survived for the sake of my children, and I live each and every day for them.

Hearing one of the kids stir, I put down my glass and head back into the holiday home, only to find April sitting up in her bed. Seeing her sleepy face makes my heart want to burst. Without a word, I curl up with her, wrapping her in a safe hug.

# Author's Note

When it was first suggested to me that I should write a book about my ordeal, I wasn't sure if I should. Seeing the details of my life plastered across newspapers was the last thing I had ever wanted or expected to happen, and it had devastated me. I am and have always been a private person, feeling uncomfortable whenever attention is thrown my way, and the prospect of my dirty laundry being aired in public felt like a nightmare.

Not only had Emile ripped my family apart but he also humiliated me. Left alone to pick up the pieces of everything he had destroyed, I was dragged into the spotlight and paraded through the headlines without a second thought to how it affected me. The trauma of everything – the fall, the trial and the intense public scrutiny – almost broke me. Even after the heavy press coverage had died down, the internet was a flurry of speculation and commentary. Every person who sent me a horrible letter through the post thought they knew what had happened better than I did.

For so long, other people have published their versions

of events, but this is my story and only I know what it was really like behind closed doors. That fateful day at the airfield, Emile had decided to silence me once and for all, but I fought back, and now I want my voice to be heard. With everyone else getting their say, I felt it was time to share my side of the story.

This has not, by any means, been an easy decision to make. Throwing myself back into the public ring was a terrifying prospect, but I hope by doing so I have better helped you to understand my life. It took me a long time to accept that what Emile was doing was domestic abuse. I had never considered myself someone who could fall for a man like the one Emile turned out to be. Sometimes it's not as obvious as a black eye or a split lip, as the stereotypes would have you believe. Emile was smarter than that. Over the years, he worked to place more and more subtle control over my life until I was completely trapped – and I didn't even know it. Thousands of women across Britain suffer under coercive and manipulative behaviour just like Emile's every day, and I want to stand as living proof that justice can be won. There was a time when I thought I would never escape the shadow Emile had cast over our family, but now I know that there is life after abuse, and the life I'm leading today is one full of hope and excitement for the future.

My husband's twisted behaviour almost killed me, but I survived. I'm not a victim. A victim would have died that day. As my parachute spiralled helplessly out of control, I could have given up. No one would have blamed me for going into shock, watching my life slip away from me as the ground came hurtling closer, but I refused to admit defeat. I fought to stay alive for the sake of my children, doing whatever it would take to make sure I'd return to the home where they waited for me. Under the same circumstances, I'd do it again. My children are my world and I'll keep fighting for them for the rest of my life.